Growing in Christ

KWABENA DONKOR

REVIEW AND HERALD® PUBLISHING ASSOCIATION
Since 1861 | www.reviewandherald.com

Scripture quotations credited to ESV are from *The Holy Bible,* English Standard Version, copyright © 2001 by Crossway Bibles, a division of Good News Publishers. Used by permission. All rights reserved.

Bible texts credited to KJV are from the King James Version of the Bible.

Scripture quotations marked NASB are from the *New American Standard Bible,* © 1960, 1962, 1963, 1968, 1971, 1972, 1973, 1975, 1977, 1995 by The Lockman Foundation. Used by permission.

Texts credited to NIV are from the *Holy Bible, New International Version.* Copyright © 1973, 1978, 1984, International Bible Society. Used by permission of Zondervan Bible Publishers.

Texts credited to NKJV are from the New King James Version. Copyright © 1979, 1980, 1982 by Thomas Nelson, Inc. Used by permission. All rights reserved.

Scripture quotations marked NLT are taken from the *Holy Bible,* New Living Translation, copyright © 1996, 2004, 2007 by Tyndale Foundation. Used by permission of Tyndale House Publishers, Inc., Carol Stream, Illinois 60188. All rights reserved.

Bible texts credited to RSV are from the Revised Standard Version of the Bible, copyright © 1946, 1952, 1971, by the Division of Christian Education of the National Council of the Churches of Christ in the U.S.A. Used by permission.

Texts credited to Young are from *Young's Literal Translation of the Holy Bible.* Grand Rapids: Baker Book House, 1953.

This book was
Edited by Gerald Wheeler
Copyedited by Ted Hessel
Cover design by Emily Ford
Cover photo by Jupiterimages
Typeset: Bembo 11/12.75

PRINTED IN U.S.A.

16   15   14   13   12   5   4   3   2   1

Library of Congress Cataloging-in-Publication Data
   Growing in Christ: the way, the truth, the life / Kwabena Donkor.
     p. cm.
1. Seventh-Day Adventist—Doctrines. I. Title.
   BX6154.D56 2012
   230'.6732—dc23
                    2011040953
ISBN 978-0-8280-2639-0

DEDICATION

To Comfort, Afia, and Kwasi

Contents

Preface

This book is not written solely for theologians and scholars. I have attempted to keep the average church member in mind. Consequently, it does not indulge in extensive scholarly footnotes, complicated exegesis of texts, or deep philosophical analyses. It simply strives to bring out the beauty and logical coherence of the Christian beliefs dear to Seventh-day Adventists. For younger members of the church who may not be particularly attracted to technical treatises on Christian beliefs, this book may act as a primer on Adventist doctrine. And for anyone who has not had the courage or time to explore the foundational guiding principles of Adventist doctrines, this book provides an introduction.

To the extent that I have achieved the goals mentioned above, much of the credit goes to my daughter, Afia Donkor, who helped to make my thoughts comprehensible and accessible.

Introduction

In 2005 the Seventh-day Adventist Church voted a statement of belief called "Growing in Christ." It was a doctrinal document. Unfortunately, today doctrine has bad press. Many regard creeds, confessions of faith, and statements of fundamental beliefs the worst expression of all that is considered objectionable about doctrines: rigidity, intolerance, exclusivity, and lack of freedom. Today's resistance to doctrinal formulations is a reflection of the cultural values of contemporary society. Ours is an ecumenical environment, and we are supposed to pull together rather than talk about things that have the potential to divide. After all, people today would rather discuss different perspectives of an idea than debate "the truth" about it. Historically the nature of Christian doctrine, especially as expressed in creeds and confessions of faith, has been that of authoritative statements of belief, not mere theological opinions. But a number of people, for secular, intellectual, and ideological reasons, object to this way of looking at things. The objectivism of the modern scientific era is being replaced by the relativism of the present postmodern age.

Reservations about creeds, however, have been with us since the Protestant Reformation for a variety of reasons. While the Reformers of the sixteenth and seventeenth centuries were prepared to grant synods and councils the right to determine controversies of faith, they were at the same time careful to note that creeds that came out of such bodies could err, and indeed had done so at times.[1] The Reformers, of course, had their focus mainly on creeds from the medieval period. In noting that synods and councils could make mistakes, the Reformers paved the way for the principle that the only unerring rule of interpreting the Bible is to let the Bible interpret itself.[2]

Coming out of the Protestant tradition, Seventh-day Adventists have maintained the same caution toward creeds, not only those of the medieval period, but also those of the Reformation denominations. Our pioneers' experience with the Protestant use of creedal statements during the early days of our church led them to see creeds and confessions of faith as oppressive barriers to the acceptance of new truth.

In spite of their reservations about doctrinal formulations, neither the Reformation churches nor Seventh-day Adventists ever denied the value of having some kind of affirmation of those beliefs important to them. While Seventh-day Adventists hold on to the principle of the Bible as their only creed, they have at different points throughout their history expressed themselves on the need for a statement of their beliefs.[3] In 1850 it became necessary to distinguish Adventists of the "original faith" from other Adventists. Then in 1853 the pioneers compiled a list of basic beliefs that they developed primarily to inform Seventh Day Baptists who wanted to be acquainted with the faith of Seventh-day Adventists. Similarly, in making their 1872 pronouncement on beliefs, Adventists were declaring to the public those things that had "with great unanimity, been held by them." Although the 1931 statement sought to give government officials in Africa a better understanding of the church's work there, it was also needed to present Adventist beliefs to the world and to correct distortions of them.

When in 1980 the church, for the first time, officially voted a set of doctrinal statements, it acknowledged for *all* time the need for a statement of fundamental beliefs to meet all the various situations that previous statements had addressed. To present themselves to those outside the faith, to avoid distortions of their beliefs by detractors, to declare their unity of thought, and to take a stand on what they deem to be correct biblical teaching on relevant issues, Adventists have, officially, put out a statement of fundamental beliefs. The church does not, however, view it as a creed. This means, as the sixteenth edition of the *Seventh-day Adventist Church Manual* states clearly in its preface to the summary of the fundamental beliefs that "Seventh-day Adventists accept the Bible as their only creed and hold certain fundamental beliefs to be the teaching of the Holy Scriptures. These beliefs, as set forth here, constitute the church's understanding and expression of the teaching of Scripture. Revision of these statements may be expected at a General Conference Session when the church is led by the Holy Spirit to a fuller understanding of Bible truth or finds better language in which to express the teachings of God's Holy Word."

However, we should not mistake the openness of the Adventist Church toward further development of truth for a lack of firm commitment to the doctrines it already holds. Adventists believe that the Spirit of God has led them in their doctrinal development until now, and they continue to depend on Him to open up new vistas of truth from Scripture. Yet they carefully pursue the search for new biblical insight in the light of the following counsel:

"When the power of God testifies to what is truth, the truth is to stand forever as the truth. No after suppositions, contrary to the light God has given are to be entertained. Men will arise with interpretations of Scripture which are to them truth, but which are not truth. The truth for this time, God has given us as a foundation for our faith. He Himself has taught us what is truth. One will arise and still another with new light which contradicts the light that God has given under the demonstration of His Holy Spirit. A few are still alive who passed through the experience gained in the establishment of this truth. God has graciously spared their lives to repeat and repeat till the close of their lives, the experience through which they passed even as did John the apostle till the very close of his life. And the standard bearers who have fallen in death, are to speak through the reprinting of their writings. I am instructed that thus voices are to be heard. They are to bear their testimony as to what constitutes the truth for this time. We are not to receive the words of those who come with a message that contradicts the special points of our faith. They gather together a mass of Scripture, and pile it as proof around their asserted theories. This has been done over and over again during the past fifty years. And while the Scriptures are God's Word, and are to be respected, the application of them, if such application moves one pillar of the foundation that God has sustained these fifty years, is a great mistake. He who makes such an application knows not the wonderful demonstration of the Holy Spirit that gave power and force to the past messages that have come to the people of God."[4]

Yet Ellen G. White balances her counsel with another, one promoting an attitude of continual searching, truth-seeking, and exploration of Adventist beliefs:

"Truth is eternal, and conflict with error will only make manifest its strength. We should never refuse to examine the Scriptures with those who, we have reason to believe, desire to know what is truth. Suppose a brother held a view that differed from yours, and he should come to you, proposing that you sit down with him and make an investigation of that point in the Scriptures; should you rise up, filled with prejudice, and condemn his ideas, while refusing to give him a candid hearing? The only right way would be to sit down as Christians, and investigate the position presented, in the light of God's work, which will reveal truth and unmask error. To ridicule his ideas would not weaken his position in the least if it were false, or strengthen your position if it were true. If the pillars of our faith will not stand the test of investigation, it is time that we knew it. There must be no spirit of Phariseeism cherished among us."[5]

In the following chapters we will explore some of the fundamental teachings of the Seventh-day Adventist Church. Our objective is to focus on the latest addition to the body of Adventist beliefs, namely "Growing in Christ." But we can best do so by looking at some fundamental beliefs that *logically* lead to "Growing in Christ," as well as those that flow from it. The exploration of the

Adventist belief system and the newest fundamental statement of belief is necessarily linked to the great controversy motif, and is the subject of chapter 1. Of course, it involves entities and issues that we will introduce in chapter 1, but God, the key "Entity" in the spiritual conflict, and humans, the "price" of the controversy, we will explore further in chapters 2 and 3 respectively. Humanity's place in the cosmic struggle, in particular, makes the issue of salvation the central topic around which every other doctrine revolves. Still, the great controversy and the issues it involves set the stage for the nature, shape, and form that the doctrine of salvation takes. Thus the great controversy motif serves as the frame, but within it the issue of salvation holds together the different components of the Adventist belief system. Chapter 4 will look at the biblical concept of salvation. Chapter 5 examines salvation from the perspective of the "victory" obtained by Jesus, while chapters 6 and 7 will study the opportunities and challenges afforded humanity by virtue of Jesus' triumph. Together chapters 5, 6, and 7 present an extended look at the newest fundamental belief, "Growing in Christ." In chapters 8 and 9 we will explore the doctrine of the church: its nature (including the remnant and its mission) and its rites and rituals. But we should understand all of this from the perspective of the church as God's agency for the salvation of erring humanity. Chapters 10 and 11 will study the effect of salvation on a person with regard to such aspects as the law of God, stewardship, general Christian behavior, and marriage and family. In the final two chapters (12 and 13) we will focus on the sanctuary, the second coming of Christ, death and resurrection, the new earth, and the millennium, issues that will be critical to our understanding of salvation and the great controversy as history draws to a close.

---

[1] See, for example, the Westminster Confession of Faith (1646), Chapter XXXI (III, IV), in John H. Leith, ed., *Creeds of the Churches* (Atlanta: John Knox Press, 1982), p. 228.

[2] Westminster Confession, Chapter I (IX, X), in Leith, p. 196.

[3] Such statements developed in response to varying situations have received various titles: "Original Faith" (1850), "Leading Doctrines" (1854), "Covenant Resolution" (1861), "Declarations of Fundamental Principles" (1872), "Fundamental Principle" (1889), and "Fundamental Beliefs" (1931, 1980, 2005).

[4] Ellen G. White, "A Call to the Watchmen," p. 14.

[5] Ellen G. White, *Gospel Workers* (Battle Creek, Mich.: Review and Herald Pub. Assn., 1892), p. 127.

Chapter 1

The Great Controversy: The Foundation

Introduction

The great controversy motif or theme is a philosophy of history—a biblical viewpoint from which one may understand humanity's story. Although Seventh-day Adventists have made much of this notion, others have expressed similar views throughout the course of Christian history.

Brief Overview of the Great Controversy in Christian Thought

From Origen (185-254), considered one of the early Greek theologians of the church, we learn that the early Christians were aware of a cosmic conflict. In the preface to his work *De Principiis* Origen spells out particular points that he believed the apostles had clearly taught. After summarizing their teaching on the Father, the Son, and the Holy Spirit, he speaks about the soul, noting that "every rational soul is possessed of free will and volition; that it has a struggle to maintain with the devil and his angels, and opposing influences, because they strive to burden it with sins."[1] Although he affirms that the devil and his angels and the opposing influences "exist indeed," Origen notes that Scripture does not clearly explain their nature and manner of existence. Nevertheless, he knew it to be the commonly held opinion that "the devil was an angel, and that, having become an apostate, he induced as many of the angels as possible to fall away with himself, and these up to the present time are called his angels."[2]

Toward the end of his life Augustine of Hippo (354-430), the most prominent of the Latin Church Fathers, wrote a work that comprised 22 books called the *The City of God*. In its last 12 books he depicted two cities, the heavenly (made up of God and His angels and His people) and the earthly (composed of the devil and his angels and wicked people). The cities, the result of "the difference that arose among the angels,"[3] depicted the battle between good and evil, and Augustine's work was designed, in part, to offer reassurance to Christians that ultimately the city of God will triumph.

Among Protestant Reformers, John Calvin knew that the wicked nature shared by Satan and his angels was the result of a conscious, deliberate revolt against the rule of God. Calvin was keenly aware of the devil's activity in a real strife with the Lord and His people. He writes concerning the devil, "Truth he assails with lies, light he obscures with darkness. The minds of men he involves in error; he stirs up hatred, inflames strife and war, and all in order that he may overthrow the kingdom of God, and drown men in eternal perdition with himself."[4]

The period following the Reformers saw a gradual reserve about the devil and angels in general, until the liberalism of the modern period dismissed them completely. Individuals such as René Descartes (1596-1650) and John Locke (1632-1704) would say only that the existence and character of the angels were unknowable, but later modern and postmodern persons, including "many evangelical Protestants have put angels and angelology out of sight and out of mind."[5]

The Great Controversy in Adventist Thought

In all of Christian history those who acknowledged some form of conflict between the forces of good and the forces of evil did not place much theological value on the idea. Augustine's *City of God* could be an exception, but none have examined the idea in such systematic detail as Seventh-day Adventists. In other words, Adventists are unique in relating the conflict between God and Satan to key biblical ideas such as the character of God, the origin of sin, the atonement of Christ, the work of the Holy Spirit, the law of God, the destiny of humanity, and the course that the plan of salvation will take beyond the second coming of Christ. When the church made the great controversy concept into a fundamental belief and included it in the Adventist Statement of Fundamental Beliefs in 1980, the church was no doubt recognizing the theological significance of the cosmic conflict. Already, as formulated in 1980, we see how the conflict touches other biblical doctrines. We note some of the biblical ideas connected with the conflict italicized in the statement of belief as quoted below:

"All humanity is now involved in a great controversy between Christ and Satan regarding the *character of God*, His *law*, and His *sovereignty* over the universe. This conflict originated in heaven when a created being, endowed with *freedom of choice*, in self-exaltation became Satan, God's adversary, and led into rebellion a portion of the angels. He *introduced the spirit of rebellion* into this world when he led Adam and Eve into sin. This human sin resulted in the distortion of the *image of God in humanity*, the disordering of the created world, and its eventual devastation at the time of the worldwide flood. Observed by the whole creation, this world became the arena of the universal conflict, out of which the *God of love will ultimately be vindicated*. To assist His people in this controversy, Christ sends the Holy Spirit and the loyal angels to guide, protect, and sustain them in the *way of salvation*. (Rev. 12:4-9; Isa. 14:12-14; Eze. 28:12-18; Gen. 3; Rom. 1:19-32; 5:12-21; 8:19-22; Gen. 6-8; 2 Peter 3:6; 1 Cor. 4:9; Heb. 1:14.)"[6]

How did a "cosmic conflict worldview" become such a hallmark of Adventist thought? Ellen G. White appears to have started a systematic clarification of the great controversy motif about the middle of the nineteenth century. At that time she presented to the Sabbatarian Adventists a work titled *Spiritual Gifts: The Great Controversy Between Christ and His Angels, and Satan and His Angels*. Out of the volume developed the well-known Conflict of the Ages Series. The first four volumes in the series trace the struggle from Genesis to Revelation. The fifth volume, titled *The Great Controversy Between Christ and Satan*, traces "the history of the controversy in past ages, and especially so to present it as to shed a light on the fast-approaching struggle of the future."[7]

Adventists have continued to reflect on "the history of the controversy in past ages" since the days of Ellen White. We wish to look at Adventist thinking on the great controversy today from the following perspectives: (1) the war that began in heaven and continues on earth; (2) the personalities and issues involved, and (3) the ways and means by which the opposing sides pursue it until the conflict is finally resolved.

The Controversy and Its Players

Revelation 12:7 quite clearly brings out the idea of a primeval war in heaven: "And there was war in heaven. Michael and his angels fought against the dragon, and the dragon and his angels fought back" (NIV). At its beginning the conflict involved Satan and his angels warring against Christ and His angels. But when we read the passage in its context, we see two perspectives about this war: a heavenly and an earthly. In Revelation 12:4 the dragon (identified in verse 9 as the devil and Satan) flings some stars (angels) to the earth, while in verse 9 Satan and his angels get cast to the earth. What is said in verses 10-12 shows that the casting out in verse 9 is somehow connected with Calvary and the victory gained over the devil through the blood of Christ. As a matter of fact, it is the "expulsion" of the devil following the cross event that causes him to resolve to go after the Christian church (verse 13). So verse 4 occupies a special place in the whole account. It seems that while John in Revelation 12:9-12 focuses on a decisive battle won against the devil on the cross, he flashes back to the primeval conflict in heaven (verse 4) to provide a point of reference for the war at the cross.

The connection John makes between the primeval struggle in heaven and the war at the cross provides several valuable insights on the great controversy motif. When John identifies the dragon as the "old serpent" he is clearly connecting him with the Garden of Eden. Here is the big picture that John seems to be painting: the war that began in heaven was reenacted here on earth in the Garden of Eden when the serpent tempted the woman, Eve. It is the same war that in due course renewed at the cross, and it is the same hostility that will be directed at the prophetic woman, the church, as depicted in verse 13. The opposing personalities are the same: God and His angels versus Satan and his angels. Humanity enters the conflict as a significant prize for them to win. To gain the allegiance of humanity, Satan deceived Adam and Eve in the garden. Christ's mission on earth, including His work through the church, was the highest expression of God's plans to regain the fallen human race. For this reason, the church eventually becomes the object of Satan's attacks.

The Bible's depiction of the conflict speaks to the situation of *real* human beings. In the same vein, God, the devil, and angels are also real and literal beings. We live in a time when people may use terms such as the devil, or angels, or even God, when they mean something very different from what we usually attach to those words. For example, some focus only on the positive roles that the word "God" may perform in human culture and society. They are not interested whether a personal God exists or not. But biblical teaching regards all these entities as real, and the great controversy motif treats them as actual beings engaged in mortal conflict. Most of the Adventist doctrines we will study in this book will not make sense if the players identified in the controversy are not real beings.

Lucifer's Fall and the Issues in the Conflict

The Bible does not explicitly spell out why the conflict started between God and Satan and where it is headed, but certain passages in Scripture allow us to make reasonable inferences. Isaiah 14:4-21 and Ezekiel 28:12-19, while set in a human context and representing the pagan kings of Tyre and Babylon, on closer inspection provide details that seem to go beyond those ancient Near Eastern rulers. They point to the origin, position, and moral fall of Satan. After his analysis of the different elements of Ezekiel 28:12-17, Lamar Eugene Cooper remarks that "the conclusion that the figure behind the poetic symbol is the serpent (also known as the adversary, the devil, Satan; Rev. 12:9) is a logical one."[8]

The texts cited above raise at least three issues that motivated Satan: pride, autonomy, and independence. The passages picture a created, dependent being aspiring to be self-sufficient and independent. But independence is always independence *from* something or somebody. First John 3:8 says that the devil has sinned from the beginning, possibly alluding to Satan's fall, and 1 John 3:4 defines sin as *lawlessness*. From these two verses we can conclude that Satan's sin, which manifested itself as a quest for independence and autonomy, represented a desire on his part to free himself from the "restraints" of the *law* of heaven—*the law of God*. Furthermore, by refusing to accept the authority of divine law, Satan indicated that he preferred to live under a different set of conditions. It seems that for him the system of laws in heaven was not ideal—even defective. But since heaven's law is a reflection of God's character, a defect in the law would amount to a defect in the divine character. Put simply, Satan's rebellion was fundamentally against God Himself.

God's Weapon and Satan's Fight

Genesis 3:15 cryptically captures the future course of the conflict that Isaiah and Ezekiel depicted. Here we have a hint of God's "rules of engagement" in the conflict between the initial participants and their followers. History has shown that ultimately Genesis 3:15 was a prophetic depiction of a conflict that climaxed in a mortal clash between Satan and a male descendant of the woman. God's weapon of choice was Jesus, who would come to fight on behalf of the woman, suffer "bruises," but ultimately deliver a deadly blow to the serpent. The plan of attack was an act of sacrifice by Jesus—a demonstration of selfless love. The weapon was fitting for the goal of the conflict—the salvation of humanity. In all of its manifestations in the course of the history of salvation, God's "weapon" has not been one that simply vanquishes the foe but that invites, wins, and causes the opponent to surrender. Whether during the time of the patriarchs, in Israel's sanctuary sacrificial rituals and prophetic activity, Christ's ministry in His death on the cross, in the work of the church, and in Christ's ministry in the heavenly sanctuary, God's love has progressively manifested itself, and all for the salvation of fallen humanity.

Throughout the ongoing conflict, God by His actions has shown His love for humanity. But Satan has attempted to counteract and nullify every manifestation of divine redemptive love toward sinful humanity. God designed the sacrificial system to remind humanity of the Creator and to keep the hope of redemption alive. Satan, through idolatry and pagan worship, opposed God so determinedly that, were it not for the preservation of a faithful remnant throughout Israel's history, he would have succeeded in bringing the Hebrew nation to total ruin (Rom. 1:20-28; Deut. 32:17, 18). After His death and resurrection Christ established His church to proclaim the good news of salvation to lost humanity. From its inception Satan has determined to weaken and destroy the church (see Acts 5:17, 18; 7:54-60; 2 Thess. 2:1-4; 1 Tim. 4:1; 2 Peter 2:1; Rev. 12:13-17). After His ascension Christ entered the heavenly sanctuary (Heb. 4:14-16; 9:24) to perform His priestly function on behalf of sinful humanity (Heb. 7:27). Yet, as we see in Daniel 8:11-14, Satan actively attempts to usurp that ministry.

Destinies

At the center of the great controversy is the choice that individuals make, especially the kind that Joshua set before the children of Israel: "And if it seems evil to you to serve the Lord, choose for yourselves this day whom you will serve, whether the gods which your fathers served that were on the other side of the River, or the gods of the Amorites, in whose land you dwell. But as for me and my house, we will serve the Lord" (Joshua 24:15, NKJV).

Prophecy gives us a view of the significant choices that will confront humanity in the closing scenes of the conflict between God and Satan. For a period of 1260 years (Dan. 7:25; 12:7; Rev. 11:2; 12:14; 13:5), Satan sporadically but persistently persecuted God's people. In the final showdown sketched in Revelation 12 and 13 the devil employs two earthly powers—a leopard-like beast (Rev. 13:1-10) and a two-horned beast (verses 11-17)—to attempt to disrupt and undermine the work of God. On His part God, before the close of the conflict, clarifies the issues involved through a three-pronged message represented in Revelation 14. Humanity needs to be intelligently informed in order for it to make up its mind about them. In the final conflict there will be people who stand loyal to God. Revelation 14 symbolizes them by the number 144,000, possibly representative of an innumerable people from all the nations of the earth (cf. Rev. 7:9-17). They will remain obedient to the commandments of God in a time of great distress, and will be wholeheartedly devoted to the worship of the Creator-God. Receiving the approval of God, they will be victorious with Him. But others will oppose God and perish in the ensuing harvest (Rev. 14:14-20). The controversy will soon come to an end. What side will you choose?

---

[1] Origen, *De Principiis,* in Alexander Roberts and James Donaldson, eds., *Anti-Nicene Fathers* (Peabody, Mass.: Hendrickson, 1999), vol. 4, p. 240.

[2] *Ibid.*

[3] Augustine, *The City of God,* trans. Marcus Dods, in Philip Schaff, ed., *Nicene and Post-Nicene Fathers* (Peabody, Mass.: Hendrickson, 1999), First Series, vol. 2, p. 205.

[4] John Calvin, *The Institutes of the Christian Religion,* Vol. I, Book XIV, chap. 15.

[5] Stephen F. Noll, "Angels," in Kevin J. Vanhoozer, ed., *Dictionary for Theological Interpretation of the Bible* (Grand Rapids: Baker Academic, 2005), p. 47.

[6] In *Handbook of Seventh-day Adventist Theology,* ed. Raoul Dederen (Hagerstown, Md.: Review and Herald Pub. Assn., 2000), p. 1001.

[7] Ellen G. White, *The Great Controversy Between Christ and Satan* (Mountain View, Calif.: (Pacific Press Pub. Assn., 1911), p. xi.

[8] Lamar E. Cooper, *Ezekiel,* The New American Commentary (Nashville: Broadman and Holman Publishers, 1994), vol. 17, p. 268.

Chapter 2

Revelation and
the God Revealed in It

Introduction

Two words primarily determine our understanding of the word "revelation" as used in Scripture: the Greek words *apokalupsis* and *phaneroun*. They tell us that revelation involves an unveiling, uncovering, or manifestation of something or someone previously concealed or covered. The previous chapter *uncovered* for us a lot of material concerning the great controversy or spiritual war that began in heaven, continues today, and will be resolved when Jesus comes the second time. That material came from the Bible.

Christians have always believed that we can learn about God from nature, history, and human conscience, but the Bible is the key source of knowledge about Him. To the extent that Scripture unveils God's nature, His will, and His ways, it has been customary to identify the Bible with revelation.[1] As we shall see, it is vital for us to be sure that the God of the controversy is the God of the Bible. But why put such a premium on Scripture, anyway? Because its self-witness compels us to see it as more than an ordinary human composition. It claims inspiration for itself, and in this chapter we focus on what the Bible says about itself and about the nature of the God revealed in it.

The Doctrine of Scripture

The word "doctrine" basically means "teaching." Therefore, when the Bible itself becomes the focus of study, the doctrine of Scripture refers to what the Bible *teaches* about itself: its origin, its trustworthiness, and its authority.

21

Two passages are of critical importance in any understanding of what the Bible declares about itself: 2 Timothy 3:14-17 and 2 Peter 1:16-21.

In 2 Timothy 3:14-17 Paul encourages Timothy to continue in the truths of salvation that he has learned from the Bible, and affirms Timothy's great advantage in having been instructed from his infancy in the saving truths of the sacred Scriptures. For Paul, such scriptures have incomparable greatness because of their divine origin. The word Paul uses to describe it, *theopneustos*, has been variously translated—"given by inspiration of God" (KJV), "inspired by God" (NASB), and "God-breathed" (NIV). The NIV comes closest to the idea that the word tries to communicate, namely, that Scripture is "breathed out by God" or "God-breathed" in the sense that it is the end product of God's creative breath. The word *does not* explain the process that produced Scripture, but it seeks to convey that God has operated within it to create the Bible.

In Scripture the breath of God serves as a symbol of His mighty power— it is God's breath that carries the power of the word that creates. Thus it was by the breath of God's mouth that He made the heavens and everything in them (Ps. 33:6). Paul's use of *theopneustos* therefore suggests that the same energy that brought the world into existence also created the Scriptures.

Second Peter 1:16-21 builds on Paul's point. Here Peter is keen to tell his readers that when they were informed about the power and coming of the Lord, it did not originate from "cunningly devised fables" (verse 16, KJV). What they received was eyewitness testimony. Better yet, this testimony was corroborated by the "more sure word of prophecy" (*ton prophetikon logon,* verse 19, KJV), not just the specific prophetic sections of the Bible, but the whole of it. The prophetic word was "more sure," because it came from people who spoke as they were "borne" (verse 21, Young) by the Holy Spirit, and was not the result of human investigation into the nature of things. Therefore, Peter emphatically denies that the Scriptures originated in the human mind and strongly asserts that God is its only source. Here we receive a slight hint of *how* Scripture was generated. It was produced through an *action* of the Holy Spirit on the human instrumentalities described as being "borne or carried." The Greek verb for "carry" appears twice in verse 21 in the passive form, and Acts 27:15, 17 employs the same verb to describe a ship propelled by a wind. While we must not press the analogy too far, we cannot miss the picture of the prophets being under the influence of God in order to convey His word.

Both Paul and Peter wanted to emphasize the authority of Scripture based on its origin and nature. Clearly the fact that God did not leave the human writers to their own devices has to count for something. The authority of the writers of the Bible is somehow connected to the fact that they were recipients of divine revelation, and we find this reality reinforced by Jesus' own attitude toward Scripture as an authoritative document (see Matt. 4:4, 7, 10; 22:41-46; John 10:33-35; 2 Peter 3:2).

Inspiration of Scripture

None of the passages previously discussed describe in unequivocal detail the process of inspiration and God's revelation to the Bible writers. In attempting to understand the nature of inspiration, some have focused on problematic sections of the Bible. Consider, for example, the wording of the inscription above Jesus' cross as depicted in the Gospels. According to Matthew, it said, "This is Jesus the King of the Jews." Mark records it as "The King of the Jews," and Luke presents it as "This is the King of the Jews." How should we relate to the differences?

Our discussion on the doctrine of Scripture should help us. First, we should begin with what the Bible has established—that all Scripture is inspired and trustworthy. Second, inspiration permits different expressions of an idea or event to the extent that they *adequately* depict the event. Where an approximation is an adequate expression, as in the inscriptions on the cross, inspiration accommodates it. But when specificity is required, as in 1 Kings 6:1, inspiration provides it. One of Ellen White's comments on inspiration is particularly relevant to this issue: "It is not the words of the Bible that are inspired, but the men that were inspired. Inspiration acts not on the man's words or his expressions but on the man himself, who, under the influence of the Holy Ghost, is imbued with thoughts. But the words receive the impress of the individual mind. The divine mind is diffused. The divine mind and will is combined with the human mind and will; thus the utterances of the man are the word of God."[2]

We should come to the Bible with a humble attitude for many reasons, especially when we confront what critics of the Bible have branded as contradictions or errors. When approaching Scripture, we should accept that we do not know everything. It means that we may need to suspend judgment on issues that we are prone to declare as contradictions or even errors. A century or so ago scholars did not believe that the Sargon of Isaiah 20:1 existed—but not so anymore! The comparison between Acts 1:18 and Matthew 27:5 is another "evidence" of what critics of the Bible claimed to be conflicting accounts of Judas' death. In this case, the word translated "falling headlong" in Acts 1:18 that in the past seemed to create a discrepancy with Matthew's account of Judas' death in 27:5 does not pose that problem anymore. Research during the twentieth century revealed that the word also means "swelling up." Therefore, it is entirely possible that after hanging himself, Judas was not discovered until his corpse bloated from decomposition, which caused his bowels to burst open. The point is, what at first seemed to be contradictory is now shown not to be.

The Mystery of the Triune God

It is important that we seek to grasp how inspiration works. But a deep understanding of how the Bible was written or even a profound appreciation of the truths revealed in it mean nothing if we do not know for ourselves the God revealed in it—the God who is at the center of the great controversy.

One thing that the Bible explicitly affirms about God is His oneness (see Deut. 6:4 and Mark 12:29). But, while affirming God's oneness, the Bible at the same time first hints at (see for example, Gen. 1:26; 3:22; 11:7; Isa. 6:8) and then later clarifies the plurality of the inner life of *the one* God. Much of this is quite difficult for us to wrap our minds around. What is clear, however, is that the expression of the oneness of God in the Bible precludes any idea of many separate deities. From the perspective of the Bible, if we are to speak of the nature of that reality that we call *divine,* it is *one* divine being and not *many* divine beings. However, the total picture we get from the Bible is that there is an inner "content" of plurality to this divine Being, even in His oneness. In a telling passage in Genesis 16 Hagar identifies the angel of the Lord as Yahweh (verse 13). Yet the angel of the Lord, identified as Yahweh, refers to Yahweh in the third person in verse 11! The Old Testament's suggestion of plurality provides hints about the inner Trinitarian being of God. Several New Testament passages, however, prepare us to consider a deeper understanding of God's being (see in particular John 1:1-3, 18; 20:28; 1 Cor. 12:4-6; 2 Cor. 13:14; 2 Peter 1:1; 1 John 5:20). This much seems clear: in the inner being of God, Jesus Christ the Son is God. Notice also that 1 Corinthians 12:4-6 and 2 Corinthians 13:14 link the Holy Spirit with the other divine Beings in a Trinitarian manner. Thus the Bible declares the inner being of the one divine reality as the Father, Son, and Holy Spirit.

One comes away from such discussions with the sense that there is a lot about God's nature that we do not fully understand and probably never will. But we may learn something, however, from how Jesus *progressively* revealed the existence of the Holy Spirit as a divine person (see John 14:1-3, 16, 17; 16:4-7, 13; Luke 24:49; Acts 1:4, 5, 8). The information the Bible gives about God, including His triune nature, is not provided for speculative philosophizing but to further our understanding of His activities, especially His redemptive work in our behalf as the great controversy unfolds and finally concludes.

The Attributes of Our Creator

God's attributes are the characteristics of His nature, the inalienable qualities that make Him God. Although the Bible reveals to us these truths about God, it does not approach them in a speculative manner, as if we can analyze them in an abstract fashion.

While the Bible spends a great deal of time teaching us about what God is like, particularly as His interaction with fallen humanity reveals His character, it spends no time trying to prove that He exists. Instead, Scripture simply assumes the existence of God without any burden to prove or show it (Gen. 1:1). It then encourages us to accept the revelation of God's existence (Heb. 11:6; Rom. 10:17). From the biblical point of view, conviction about the existence of God cannot be had through rational arguments. The Bible teaches that a person accepts the reality of God's existence through personal experience with Him as the Holy Spirit *through the Bible* impresses that individual's heart and mind with the fact of His existence.

We can define God's attributes several different ways. Some of them, such as love, are qualities partially found in humanity. Others, such as omnipresence, have no human counterpart. Sometimes we make a distinction between those characteristics, such as His essence as Spirit, which remain within God's own nature, and those, such as His mercy, which work outside of divine nature as He relates to His creation.

One easier way to categorize God's attributes is to distinguish what we can refer to as His *natural* attributes from His *moral* ones. God's natural attributes are the superior nonmoral qualities He has, such as His essence as Spirit and His invisible quality (John 4:24), His infinity (present everywhere/every time and limitless, Ps. 139:7-12), and His constancy (Ps. 102:26, 27; Mal. 3:6; James 1:17). God's moral attributes are those qualities that, from a human perspective, relate to issues of rightness or wrongness. Among them are His purity (holiness, righteousness, and justice [see Isa. 6:1-4; Jer. 9:24]); His integrity (genuineness, truthfulness, and faithfulness [see John 17:3; 1 Sam. 15:29; and 1 Thess. 5:24]); and His love (benevolence, grace, and mercy [see John 3:16; Ex. 34:6; Ps. 103:13]).

It is absolutely vital in examining God's attributes that we do not reduce it to a philosophical exercise. Instead, their study should be an attempt to understand, from the Bible and within the context of the great controversy, the nature of the God on whose side we stand. The Lord is actively involved with His creation in bringing about His purposes in the midst of a real conflict. The more we grasp of His character and recognize its display in everyday life, the greater our trust in the goodness and reliability of His character will grow. We confirm His reality and existence and strengthen our faith and dependence on Him as the great controversy unfolds.

The Activities of God

We find both distinctiveness and relatedness between the activities of the mind and body. While seemingly operating in two separate spheres, each is nevertheless controlled and informed by the other. For instance, our mental activity directs our physical activity. Something similar can be said about God's activities. His physical/concrete actions are preceded by His mental/spiritual activities. God's mental/spiritual activities are unique to His Godhood, and we can divide them into two categories: foreknowledge and predestination. They work hand in hand to set the stage for God's physical/concrete actions. Foreknowledge is the biblical name for God's prior knowledge of things before they happen (Ps. 139:1-5; Isa. 40:28; Job 37:16; Heb. 4:13; Rom. 8:29). Predestination, as presented in Ephesians 1:5, 9, 11; 1 Corinthians 2:7; and Romans 8:29, means "to decide beforehand," and is treated as an *act* of the will on God's part. As mentioned before, the two concepts work hand in hand. In having the capacity to know things beforehand (foreknowledge),

God is able to plan ahead and implement a course of action to deal with circumstances before they happen (predestination). Concerning the Fall of humanity, God's foreknowledge caused Him to make a provision for the salvation of humanity (predestination) even before He created the earth. That is why Scripture tells us that Jesus Christ was slain from the foundation of the world (Rev. 13:8). With the plan in place, each individual may freely respond to the provision for salvation in Jesus Christ.

When we think about the concrete activities of God, His *creation* readily comes to mind (Gen. 1; 2; Ps. 33:6; Rom. 4:17; Heb. 11:3). The Bible presents creation as something brought into being from "nothing." It is the separate and distinct result of God's creative work and not an emanation or extension of His infinite being—a vital point to keep in mind. Although God is infinite and limitless, it is possible for entities to exist outside of Him. Ideas about God that try to make Him a part of nature (pantheism or panentheism) clearly miss the mark. The Lord stands distinct from the creation and yet is involved in it to *preserve* it (Neh. 9:6) and *govern* its history, whether through direct intervention (Ex. 3:1-14) or indirect involvement (Matt. 9:8; cf. Acts 14:15, 16).

Why the Doctrine of Revelation and the God Revealed in It Matters

Seventh-day Adventists understand all biblical truths in the light of the great controversy motif. At the center of the conflict is God. Not the God of the philosophers or that of science, but the God of the Bible. The credibility of the great controversy message and the Deity who is at the center of it is critically linked to the truth of the biblical Word. If we cannot trust the Bible on these issues, then nothing we say about them matters. But if the Bible is God's revealed Word, then we can be sure that we stand on firm ground. The knowledge that the Bible provides about the nature, attributes, and activities of God is of the utmost importance as believers take their stand on the side of God in the struggle between good and evil.

---

[1] It is true that some today take the view that the Bible is *only* a witness to revelation, thereby wishing to distance revelation from text. Yet Stephen William's assessment of revelation's relation to the text is in the main accurate: "It is evident that Scripture bears witness to revelation. But we must go further than this.... From the perspective of the Bible itself, the text can and should be regarded as the word of God. Whether the Bible as a whole is to be considered the word of God, and what we should make of ecclesiastical disagreements on what constitutes the Bible, are further questions. But the spoken word of God can be textually inscribed and enjoy in salient respects the same status of revelation, even when its originating accompaniments have disappeared." See Stephen N. Williams, "Revelation," in K. J. Vanhoozer, ed., *Dictionary for Theological Interpretation of the Bible*, pp. 679, 680.

[2] Ellen G. White, *Selected Messages* (Washington, D.C.: Review and Herald Pub. Assn., 1958), book 1, p. 21.

Chapter 3

Humanity: God's Handiwork

Introduction

A nineteenth-century thinker, Arthur Schopenhauer, while deep in thought, accidentally bumped into someone on the street. The offended person angrily said, "Who do you think you are?" To which Schopenhauer responded, "Who am I? How I wish I knew."

We should know the biblical teaching about human beings for at least two key reasons. First, it is important because of its relationship to other major biblical teachings. After all, the gospel and all its related teachings, including that of the great controversy, are directed toward humanity. Second, at a time when many intellectual disciplines focus on the study of human beings, Bible-believing people ought to know the biblical perspective. No other biblical teaching is as critical to our understanding of humans as is the teaching on creation, because it focuses on the *origin* of humans and not merely on the *beginning* of the human race. "Beginning" may refer simply to the fact of coming to be, but the word "origin" brings forth the idea of *purpose* or the why that human beings came into being. Because biblical creation focuses on origins, it paves the way for our study of humans.

Creation and Human Origins

Genesis 1:27 gives the basic facts about humanity's origins: "So God created man in His own image; in the image of God He created him; male and female He created them" (NKJV). The presence of a Creator and a conscious act of creation evidences *purpose*. If acknowledged, the fact of our creation and the reality of a Creator deny the argument that humans come with no inherent meaning or purpose and are therefore free to provide their own. As the evangelical theologian Stanley Grenz observed: "The statement 'God is our origin' affirms that God is the source or the ground of the essence called 'human.' . . . It is not true that we must each create whatever meaning we can, or that we must devise our own essence through the choices we make. On the contrary, God has designed human kind with a purpose in view. Therefore, there is an objectively true human essence which God calls each human being to acknowledge, reflect, and actualize in life."[1]

The biblical view about our origin is radically different from, and even contradictory to, other concepts of human origin such as evolution. Essence implies purpose, but evolutionary thinking is ultimately purposeless. According to the Bible, God made us in His image and He created us to bring glory to Him.

The Image of God: Part 1

When we speak about origins we are dealing with history, and that is how the Bible sees human origin (see Jude 14; Rom. 5:12-21; 1 Cor. 15:20-22). We can dismiss the historicity of Adam only by distorting the plain reading of the biblical text. It seems quite clear from Scripture that Adam and Eve were literal people, "made in the image of God," and not mere symbols or mythical figures. Our immediate sense is that being made in the image of God appears to be good, but what does that really mean?

The concept of the image of God has been defined in many ways. A common interpretation takes God's "image in man" to mean the "properties" or qualities that constitute a person as a human being. In the course of Christian history those who have followed such an approach have ended up narrowing it down to the notion of reason, namely, the intellectual dimension of human beings. Although we find some truth to it, such an approach does have its problems. For example, are we to suppose that since intelligence varies from person to person, the more intellectual a person is, the higher the extent to which the image of God is present in that individual? Certainly not.

Careful attention to the text of Genesis 1:26 demonstrates a statement of *intention* that seems to be linked to the creation of humanity in God's image. God creates them in His image and then commands them to have dominion. The creation in God's *image* appears to be necessary for the *function*—therefore, the image appears to point to the physical, intellectual, social, and spiritual endowments that would be needed for humanity to fulfill God's purpose for it.

God's image is not something that humanity has or does. Instead, it points to the very nature and essence of being human. Moreover, having the image of God is critical to our God-given task of having "dominion over" the rest of the creation, which, at the very least, entailed exercising respect, care, and good stewardship over God's creation. In doing so, humanity was to reflect to the rest of creation God's own interaction with humans. Humans were to *re-present* God to the world. And what an awesome responsibility that is!

Jesus' encounter with the Pharisees and Herodians reported in Mark 12:13-17 opens up another helpful dimension to the concept of the "image of God." While the expression does not appear in the passage, we can still readily observe here a teaching about God's image in humanity. Jesus' message seems to be "Give your money to Caesar; it has his image on it, and thus it belongs to him. But give yourselves to God. You bear his image, and you belong to him."[2] Stated practically, we show that we bear God's image through our love, commitment, and loyalty to Him, and in how we treat others and the rest of God creation. We primarily demonstrate our reflection of God's image through our actions. As Stanley Grenz perceptively notes, "we are in the image of God insofar as we have received, are now fulfilling, and one day will fully actualize a divine design. And this design—God's intent for us—is that we mirror for the sake of creation the nature of the creator."[3]

The Image of God: Part 2

Because we are human beings made in the image of God and destined to fulfill a God-given purpose, He has endowed us with physical, intellectual, social, and spiritual capabilities. They point to something integral, to who we are as humans—people created for relationships both toward God and toward each other. Humanity's relationship to God is the first and most fundamental relationship. It is impossible for humans to fulfill their God-given purpose without cultivating a right relationship with Him. God imprints His image within us. If we are to reflect His image to creation, we must be connected—mind, body, and soul—to Him. When in Genesis 3:8 we find the human pair hiding from God, we are witnessing a connection with God that has broken, resulting in a consequential abandonment of responsibility. No longer engaged in the work He placed them in the garden to do, the couple is instead distracted by the shame and guilt brought on by their betrayal.

Humanity's relationship to other humans is the second important aspect worthy of exploration. That between Adam and Eve, based on unity, intimacy, mutual fellowship, and love, forms the initial and foundational example of God's ideal for human relationships of every kind. God brought the first man and woman together, and by His command, the whole earth was filled with their offspring. It was God's will that humans come together and share with each other the blessing of mutual fellowship and love.

Unfortunately the world has strayed from the ideal expressed in the creation of Adam and Eve. We deal today with contemporary issues of racism, injustice, war, homelessness, poverty, and other social challenges. As we attempt to grapple with them it is important that we not lose sight of our origin. Sharing a common humanity and a common parentage, we were created to live together in fellowship and love. Most important, we have the image of God imprinted within us and the solemn duty to reflect it to the rest of the world.

A Defiled Image

Violence, suffering, and death surround us on every side. Evolution accepts this as a necessary part of life–a reality that has been with us from the very beginning. That would be a fitting conclusion if life, as we know it, were the result of natural selection (survival of the fittest). But such an explanation does not fit the biblical view, and a marriage of evolutionary philosophy with the biblical perspective of God and creation would end in absurdity and leave a negative impression of God's character. After all, what kind of God uses violence, selfishness, and dominance of the strong over the weak to create a progressively superior creation, and then require that creation to be redeemed from the influence of violence, selfishness, and dominance? But the Bible paints a different picture. Humanity, once created perfect, has regressed into evil and violence because of the Fall. When our first parents, Adam and Eve, committed the first sin by eating the forbidden fruit, it had a devastating and pervasive impact on the entire world (see Rom. 5:12-14), an effect that would persist until the end of earth's history. But even after the Fall, the image of God in humanity was not totally obliterated. Though humanity had sinned, the evidence that God's image still dwelt within them manifested itself in the way they related to each other (see Gen. 9:6).

Still, the introduction of sin into God's perfect creation marred His image in humanity (see Col. 3:10). Jeremiah speaks rather gravely about the condition of the human heart: "The heart is more deceitful than all else and is desperately sick; who can understand it?" (Jer. 17:9, NASB). Ellen White states that "iniquity has debased the form of human beings, and has well nigh obliterated the image of God from their hearts."[4] Sin has had a particularly devastating effect on human relationships. Competitiveness and jealousy replaced empathy and love (James 4:1, 2; Phil. 2:3-5). The experience of social alienation and estrangement is common, and the risk of physical, spiritual, and eternal death is a constant reality. Sin has even made its mark on the earth itself. Ellen White describes a "threefold" curse that rests on the world—the first from Adam's fall, the second from Cain's murder of Abel, and the third from the damage caused by the Flood. But as deep and pervasive as the effects of sin have been on humans, the situation is not altogether irreversible. The Bible speaks about the possibility of renewal and restoration of the image of God in humanity.

Restoration

Romans 8, and verses 26-30 in particular, brims with hope of restoration that is anchored in the very fabric of God's eternal plan for His creation. In verses 26, 27 Paul argues that because the Spirit who prays on behalf of believers does so *according to God's will*, His prayers are always answered. Then in verses 28-30 he draws our attention to the central goal of the Spirit's prayer: that believers, foreknown by God, have been predestined to become conformed to the image of God's Son. But the predestination Paul speaks of here does not involve the election of particular individuals to salvation. Rather, God has foreordained that believers be brought into "moral conformity to the likeness of His Son."[5] What is predestined is that we become like Christ (cf. 2 Cor. 3:18).

The Bible clearly holds up the hope for humans to be remade in God's image. The renewal of the divine image will remove the effects of sin on human relationships. Such restoration is not a human effort—it is God's work. The Bible points to Christ as the basis of the hope of human renewal. Second Corinthians 3:18 describes Christ as the means whereby God will return the divine image to fallen humanity. It is by beholding the glory of the Lord as in a glass that transforms the believer into God's image. A gradual and progressive process, it occurs in successive stages until it climaxes in the glorification portrayed in Romans 8:28-30. The transformative re-creation (2 Cor. 5:17) is made possible to those who, in the midst of spiritual warfare between the flesh and the spirit (Gal. 5:16, 17), remain watchful and diligent, and embrace the challenge in the strength of the Lord (Eph. 6:10-13). Those who choose to be remade in the image of God place themselves on His side in the ongoing great cosmic conflict. They have a special responsibility: "because this experience [of renewal] is his, the Christian is not therefore to fold his hands, content with that which has been accomplished for him. He who has determined to enter the spiritual kingdom will find that all the powers and passions of unregenerate nature, backed by the forces of the kingdom of darkness, are arrayed against him. Each day he must renew his consecration, each day do battle with evil. Old habits, hereditary tendencies to wrong, will strive for the mastery, and against these he is to be ever on guard, striving in Christ's strength for victory."[6]

Such are the marching orders of the Christian. May God help us to embrace them with cheerfulness and steadfast commitment.

---

[1] Stanley Grenz, *Theology for the Community of God* (Grand Rapids: William B. Eerdmans, 2000), p. 142.

[2] Millard Erickson, *Christian Theology* (Grand Rapids: Baker Book House, 1990), p. 515.

[3] Grenz, p. 177.

[4] Ellen G. White, *Manuscript Releases* (Silver Spring, Md.: Ellen G. White Estate, 1981-1993), vol. 9, p. 376.

[5] R. H. Mounce, *Romans*, The New American Commentary (Nashville: Broadman and Holman Pub., 2001), vol. 27, p. 189.

[6] Ellen G. White, *The Acts of the Apostles* (Mountain View, Calif.: Pacific Press Pub. Assn., 1911), pp. 476, 477.

Chapter 4

Salvation:
The Only Solution

Introduction

Scripture presents the biblical doctrine of salvation as the only solution to the sin problem. Creating anomalies in God's original creation and defiling the image of God in humanity, sin began with Lucifer's rebellion in heaven and spread to the earth through the fall of Adam and Eve. God's part in the controversy between good and evil since its beginning has been to stop—and ultimately eliminate—the deleterious effects of sin on the creation as a whole. The Christian doctrine of salvation refers to God's action to rescue the creation from sin's destructive impact.

The Scope of the Problem

We can perhaps best understand the seriousness of the sin problem only when we grasp just what it took to solve it. Because salvation is God's solution to sin, the extent of the effects of sin itself determines the scope of the solution. It must be comprehensive enough to confront the entire threat. The cross proves the utter futility of a human "solution." An extreme situation called for an extreme response—God bearing in Himself our sins and suffering the punishment we deserved.

Scholars have noted that the Old Testament alone uses about 50 specific and general Hebrew terms for sin. But the origins of three particular words are worth noting. The Hebrew root *ps* suggests to some the underlying motive for sin, namely, a refusal to submit to rightful authority. It involves willful violation of a standard. *Ht*, a more widely employed term, basically describes missing a goal. Hence in its religious sense it speaks fundamentally to humanity's departure from God's purpose. The Hebrew root word *un*, a descriptive term, appears to depict the human state as "bent" or "crooked."

Besides the indications we get from the root words used to describe sin in the Old Testament, the account of the Fall in Genesis 3 shows the effects of sin both on humans and the created world. Humanity and nature itself became corrupted. "Hostility now dominates the relationship between the woman and the serpent, between the woman and the man, between the woman and her sons. The man and the ground from which he was taken become mortal enemies."[1]

Like the Old Testament, the New Testament employs several words to portray the phenomenon of sin. The following are a few of the most common: *parabasis* describes the transgressing of a boundary; *paraptoma* denotes falling into a situation in which one should have stood upright; *agnoema* indicates ignorance about things one ought to know; *plemmeleia* points to a fundamental dissonance in the harmony of the universe. Another term, *hamartia*, together with its related verbs, is the most widely used term for sin in the New Testament. It depicts sin as a complex phenomenon. Although it may refer to specific acts, it also presents sin as a defective force inside the human person. Who among us hasn't known—deeply, personally, and painfully—just how bad the sin problem is? We live every moment of our lives with the reality of sin and its effects. To a great degree sin dominates every aspect of human existence on our planet. Not only are there problem people (Ps. 37:40; 43:1; 59:2; 2 Sam. 22:18; Luke 1:68-71) and problem situations (Ps. 34:4, 6, 17; 1 Sam. 26:24; Matt. 9:21; Luke 8:36; Heb. 2:15; 5:7), but there is also the problem of a cosmic instigator (John 16:11). From the halls of kings to the innermost recesses of the human heart, sin has infected the race. Without a divine solution, there would be none at all. How grateful we should be that God has provided the plan of salvation.

God's Provision: Carefully Planned Before the Ages

The effects of sin were immediate and needed instant attention. It was necessary, therefore, for some kind of provision to be already in place when sin manifested itself. Ellen White expressed it clearly: "As soon as there was sin, there was a Savior. Christ knew that He would have to suffer, yet He became man's substitute. As soon as Adam sinned, the Son of God presented Himself as surety for the human race, with just as much power to avert the doom pronounced upon the guilty as when He died upon the cross of Calvary."[2]

Several texts of Scripture point to the divine anticipation of the sin problem. In 1 Corinthians 2 Paul claims to "speak God's wisdom in a mystery, the hidden wisdom, which God predestined before the ages to our glory" (verse 7, NASB). The apostle does not use the word "mystery" to describe an obscure revelation inaccessible to all but a chosen elect. Rather, it is God's wisdom contrasted with human wisdom (verse 5). Paul consistently uses the word "mystery" to describe what, by human wisdom alone, can never become intelligible. It is something that humanity can know only by revelation. In this case, the subject matter of the mystery is something that God predestined *(prohorizo)* "before the ages" to the glory of sinful humanity. The word *prohorizo* expresses definite planning and careful, timely implementation. God's purpose to save was framed "before the ages" (i.e., before the beginning of time) and was not left to chance. And the wisdom that was already at work before time, unknown to human understanding but now revealed by God, is the knowledge of the gospel of a crucified Christ (verses 1, 2).

At the very beginning of Paul's Epistle to Titus he talks about the hope of eternal life that he shares with God's people. And he describes this hope as having been promised "before" the world began (Titus 1:2). From eternity God had made provision for the threat of sin (see Eph. 1:1-3; 2 Thess. 2:13, 14; Rev. 13:8). Though God did not foreordain that sin would occur, He knew that it could and had prepared to meet it. By this, God predestined the salvation of the world, and here we understand the true meaning of predestination. God planned from eternity that all human beings would have salvation in Jesus. To reject it is profoundly tragic, but it is an individual exercise of free choice. Though some may choose to turn away, it remains a provision big enough and all-encompassing enough to save everyone who desires salvation.

God's Provision in Action

Christ's sacrifice on the cross was the climax of the outworking of God's plan of salvation in the history of the world. He first articulated it as a promise: "And I will put enmity between you and the woman, and between your seed and her Seed; He shall bruise your head, and you shall bruise His heel" (Gen. 3:15, NKJV). The promise disclosed an intergenerational controversy that would ultimately result in the defeat of the serpent, Satan, by Christ, the seed of the woman (Rom. 16:20). But a fierce conflict between good and evil that began in the Garden of Eden and played out to the time of Noah's flood and beyond had first to precede Christ's victory on the cross.

At the time of Noah's flood "the wickedness of man was great in the earth, and that every intent of the thoughts of his heart was only evil continually" (Gen. 6:5, NKJV). Such relentless evil threatened humanity with extinction. But God promised to preserve life on earth, and His promise took the form of a covenant (a solemn contractual agreement).

A key underlying idea of the covenant concept is the notion of a relationship involving obligations. This is especially significant, because, in expressing His promise as a covenant, God placed such stipulations on Himself. He established an everlasting covenant with Noah, a promise of mercy for all (Gen. 6:18), and repeated the idea of the "everlasting" covenant in His covenant with Abraham (Gen. 17:7, 13), with the children of Israel at Sinai (Ex. 31:16), and with David (2 Sam. 23:5). In the midst of national ruin and exile He proclaimed an everlasting covenant promising Israel's restoration (Jer. 32:40). And in the face of sin and humanity's eternal separation from God, He made an everlasting covenant to provide Jesus as a means of salvation.

Because of the number of examples mentioned above, the Bible speaks about covenants in the plural (Rom. 9:4; Gal. 4:24). Yet each covenant was an individual component of a larger picture—an expression of God's one purpose of salvation in the promised Seed, Jesus Christ. Starting with the first gospel promise (Gen. 3:15), continuing with the early sacrificial system (Gen. 4:4), then to the covenant with Abram (Gen. 12:1-3) and the Israelite sanctuary service (Ex. 25:8), everything was to point to, and climax in, the life, death, resurrection, and heavenly ministry of Jesus Christ, God's ultimate provision to solve the sin problem.

So how should we approach God's offer of salvation? Only one response is fitting: "The only faith that will benefit us is that which embraces Him [Christ] as a personal Savior; which appropriates His merits to ourselves. Many hold faith as an opinion. Saving faith is a transaction by which those who receive Christ join themselves in covenant relation with God."[3]

God's Provision of Salvation: The Gift of Jesus Christ

As noted previously, all of God's covenants in time reached their climax in the new covenant established through the sacrificial death of Jesus Christ. Scripture presents Christ's sacrificial death as *atonement* for sin, i.e., the means by which the sin problem in all its manifestations is ultimately dealt with. But we need to explore how the death of Christ provides for humanity's need of salvation. We may examine it from the perspectives of justification, sanctification, and glorification.

Justification—The death of Christ, first of all, satisfies the human need to be reconciled to God, a step achieved through faith in the blood of Jesus Christ. Romans 3:24, 25 declares that God justifies us by His grace "through the redemption that is in Christ Jesus, whom God set forth as a propitiation by His blood, through faith" (NKJV). The word "justify" reflects a Hebrew word meaning "to be just or righteous." It involves the declaration, vindication, or restoration to the right. Justification has a forensic flavor—it accomplishes our "legal acquittal" from guilt. But because God is our Father as well as our judge, the concept of justification is not simply a rigid legal arrangement. It goes beyond cold legality and embraces the concept of grace.

Sin—disobedience to the commandment of God—cost the entire human race the right to a proper standing before Him. It introduced contempt for a holy Deity and awakened His wrath. Consequently, humanity was deserving of death. But Christ became our surety (Heb. 7:22). When the Son of God assumed our form in the Incarnation, He placed Himself in real sympathy with our sinful state, assumed responsibility for our sins, and satisfied the demands of the law by shedding His blood on Calvary. This is what it means to say that Christ's blood has atoned for our sins. And because of it, a change takes place that restores peace between the sinner and God. Something as real as the havoc that sin has wreaked on humanity renders it not a theory but an experience.

How does the blood of Christ become effective in the sinner's life? Romans 3:24, 25 makes extremely clear that justification and reconciliation (God's work) come only by faith (see Rom. 4; 5; Gal. 2:15-3:18). It is by faith that sinners accept their sinful state (Rom. 3:23), and it is by faith that the sinner receives justification as a gift from Christ (verse 24). In the parable of the Pharisee and publican, recorded in Luke 18:9-14, Jesus contrasted a proud Pharisee who vaunted his moral achievements and thanked God that he was not like other sinful people, with a publican who acknowledged his sinful state and cast himself on divine mercy. Of the two, the publican "went down to his house justified rather than the other" (verse 14, NKJV).

Sanctification—Newly justified, the repentant sinner, now united with Christ, begins to experience an inward change of character, a sanctifying work that Scripture declares to be the ultimate goal of Christ's suffering: "Therefore Jesus also, that He might sanctify the people with His own blood, suffered outside the gate" (Heb. 13:12, NKJV). Sanctification is that important! But what does it mean?

Sanctification is what happens to believers when the Holy Spirit begins to apply Christ's work on the cross to their life. It is, therefore, a continuation of the process begun in justification. The basic meaning of the word is "to make holy." Therefore, sanctification is the method by which God makes the justified sinner actually holy.

The Bible presents two aspects to the concept of sanctification, both related to holiness. The first involves the state of being separate or set apart as holy. As God told the people of Israel: "You shall be holy, for I the Lord your God am holy" (Lev. 19:2, NKJV). Similarly, Peter addressed the New Testament believers as "a chosen generation, a royal priesthood, a holy nation, His own special people" (1 Peter 2:9, NKJV). Sanctification has its beginning in the past act of justification. Thus Paul could address the Corinthians as "those who are sanctified in Christ Jesus, [and] called to be saints" (1 Cor. 1:2, NKJV). Despite the many ethical challenges the church in Corinth was facing, they were justified and had therefore embarked on the path of sanctification.

The second aspect of sanctification is moral in nature. The new relationship in which the believer is separated or set apart for God becomes meaningful only as it manifests itself concretely in a conscious following of divine will. The union in Christ that the believer experiences following justification has consequences on the moral life. One who has known justification has also been attracted by the prospect of a new life in Christ (2 Cor. 5:17). The vision of such a life becomes a divinely empowered reality that affects the believer's day-to-day activities. Biblical writers depict it as a walk with Christ or a walk according to the Spirit (Rom. 8:4, 5). The regenerative power of the Holy Spirit combats the mortal body's lingering desires. Thus the believer does not continue to live according to what Scripture calls the dictates of the flesh (Gal. 5:16-25).

But when we investigate these moral aspects of sanctification in the Bible, several ideas become evident. First, sanctification is a progressive experience. Paul could confidently assure the Philippians that "He who has begun a good work in you will complete it until the day of Jesus Christ" (Phil. 1:6, NKJV). Furthermore, as believers we "are being transformed into the same image from glory to glory, just as by the Spirit of the Lord" (2 Cor. 3:18, NKJV) as we are encouraged to "put on the new man who is renewed in knowledge according to the image of Him who created him" (Col. 3:10, NKJV). Second, sanctification is the result of a supernatural work, not human-made reform. Paul prayed, "May the God of peace Himself sanctify you completely; and may your whole spirit, soul, and body be preserved blameless at the coming of our Lord Jesus Christ" (1 Thess. 5:23, NKJV; see also Eph. 5:26; Titus 2:14; Heb. 13:20, 21). Yet sanctification is genuinely a matter of cooperation between God and the believer. Paul could say that Christ Jesus "became for us wisdom from God—and righteousness and sanctification and redemption" (1 Cor. 1:30, NKJV). At the same time, the apostle acknowledged the role of the individual when he said in Romans 8:13: "For if you live according to the flesh you will die; but if by the Spirit you put to death the deeds of the body, you will live" (NKJV). Here is no encouragement to sanctification by works. Instead, it is a simple acknowledgment of the believer's role. Believers have a biblically recognized part to play. Through Bible reading and contemplation (Ps. 1:2; Matt. 4:4; John 17:17), prayer (Eph. 6:18; Phil. 4:6), worship (Eph. 5:18-20), witnessing (Matt. 28:19, 20), and Christian fellowship (Heb. 10:24, 25),[4] believers cooperate with the Spirit and make themselves available for God's transformative work.

Glorification—Paul connects the concepts of justification and sanctification with the final crowning salvation element: glorification. God seeks to restore His relationship with His creation (Rom. 1:17). If we are to be saved, it is God who must do it. And He has made a way by planning that the gift of salvation will be made available to all who exercise faith in Jesus Christ (Rom. 3:21-26). Thus God's righteousness, which He grants to the saved, comes as a gift. To show this claim more fully, Paul speaks of Abraham's experience (Rom. 4:1-12). Having been justified by faith, Abraham experienced the first consequence of justification: "peace with God" (Rom. 5:1) and the beginning of the new relationship that develops between the Lord and those who turn to Him in faith. The next consequence of justification is an ushering into the presence of God, which is expressed as "access by faith into this grace in which we stand" (verse 2, NKJV). It leads the believer to a third result, a rejoicing in the hope of sharing the glory of God. Though by sin humanity fell short of the glory of God (Rom. 3:23), by virtue of God's provision of salvation, "we can move toward the goal he [God] had in mind in creation. The fall of humankind did not put an end to God's plans once and for all, but rather necessitated an eternally significant detour through the cross and the empty tomb. God's plan that we should reflect his glory is now being realized in the lives of obedient believers."[5] Still, Paul recognizes a future and as yet unrealized dimension to this hope. Romans 8 explains that some salvation promises have not yet come fully to pass (see verses 17, 18, 21, 39). We look forward to the restoration of the glory that Adam lost and Jesus regained.

The Experience of Salvation

The sinner is justified and reconciled on the objective basis of Christ's atoning sacrifice for all (Rom. 5:6-10). The provision that God has made for justification and reconciliation needs, however, to enter the life of the believer. It is not enough to have just a theoretical knowledge about justification. We need to experience what it means for ourselves.

From Acts 2:36-38 and Acts 3:19 we learn that repentance gives the sinner an opening to salvation. Repentance as a feeling of remorse helps us to connect the experience of justification with the death of Christ. "Nothing so touches the depths of the soul as a sense of Christ's pardoning love. When sinners contemplate this unfathomable divine love, displayed on the cross, they receive the most powerful motivation possible to repent. This is the goodness of God that leads us to repentance (Rom. 2:4)."[6]

Faith is central to salvation, and the Bible tells us that it comes by hearing, and hearing by the Word of God (Rom. 10:17). We have also seen that contemplating the love of Christ motivates a person to repentance. Repentance, then, is not the special prerogative of a privileged few. Anyone who diligently studies and prayerfully contemplates the Word of God and the sacrifice of Jesus may also share it. Everyone may receive the gift of salvation. The experience of justification places within the life of the believer spiritual realities that begin to have effects on the person's life. Justification forgives sinners (Luke 7:47; Eph. 1:7; Rom. 4:7), acquits them of charges of sin, reckons them righteous (Rom. 5:16, 18; Rom. 8:1), and gives them the gift of a new life (Eph. 2:1-5; 2 Cor. 5:17).

---

[1] David Noel Freedman, *The Anchor Bible Dictionary* (New York: Doubleday, 1992), vol. 6, p. 38.

[2] Ellen G. White, *God's Amazing Grace* (Washington, D.C.: Review and Herald Pub. Assn., 1973), p. 23.

[3] *Ibid.*, p. 140.

[4] Wayne A. Grudem, *Systematic Theology: An Introduction to Biblical Doctrine* (Grand Rapids: Zondervan Pub. House, 1994), p. 755.

[5] R. H. Mounce, *Romans*, p. 134.

[6] *Seventh-day Adventists Believe . . .*, 2nd ed. (Silver Spring, Md.: Ministerial Association, General Conference of Seventh-day Adventists, 2005), pp. 135, 136.

Chapter 5

Growing in Christ

Introduction

The amendment to the statement of fundamental beliefs voted at the fifty-eighth General Conference session of Seventh-day Adventists held in St. Louis, Missouri, was titled "Growing in Christ." It makes the following significant points: (1) Jesus has defeated satanic powers and evil forces; (2) victory over such powers, including their past manifestations in a person's life, is possible through Christ; (3) but such victory requires certain conditions. The next three chapters will deal with each point in turn. But before we address those issues, it is important to explore the nature of the victory and the salvation that Christ won for us on the cross. By understanding that victory, we can better grasp what can happen in our own lives.

Redemption

Christianity is "a religion of redemption" that saves a person from his or her condition as a sinner. The New Testament expressions for redemption derive from the word *lutron,* meaning deliverance from bondage in return for the payment of compensation or the offering of a substitute. *Lutron,* a noun, refers to the actual ransom paid for securing the freedom of a person. The redeemed individual, not in a position to free himself or herself, is released by the payment of the *lutron,* the ransom.

The New Testament uses *lutron* to portray people as enslaved to sin (John 8:34) and in desperate need of deliverance by the intervention of Another, Jesus. Thus we may distinguish Christianity from "a religion of works" in which, by "good works," a person may rectify his or her plight. From the Christian perspective, not only are those without Christ enslaved to sin, they are under a death penalty (Rom. 6:23). To be saved from their double calamity sinners require outside intervention, and that came at a price: the death of Jesus on the cross.

Embedded in the New Testament concept of redemption is the idea of substitution, an exchange. The higher the price required to effect redemption, the more redemption comes at a sacrifice. The life of Christ—the only price that could be paid for the redemption of humanity—was offered as the ultimate substitutionary exchange. Jesus took our place, sacrificing Himself in our behalf, and suffering a fate that was ours to bear. He was our ransom (Mark 10:45) and our substitute, and in His sacrifice He lived what He taught while He was on the earth: "Greater love has no one than this, that one lay down his life for his friends" (John 15:13, NASB). Christ was also the sacrifice for our sins. John the Baptist described Jesus as the Lamb of God who takes away the sins of the world (John 1:29). The verb used for sanctify, *hagiazo,* often carried sacrificial undertones. When Jesus therefore prayed, "For them I sanctify myself, that they too may be truly sanctified" (John 17:19, NIV), He conveyed the idea that His sanctification, the sacrifice of His own life, would be the means by which believers would be cleansed from sin and set apart as holy to God.

Today, some reject the concept of substitution and feel uneasy about the idea of one person suffering in place of another, particularly when that other individual is actually guilty. But this is the heart and soul of the gospel message. The fact is that "when the New Testament speaks of redemption, then, unless our linguistics are at fault, it means that Christ has paid the price of our redemption. To the extent that the price paid must be adequate for the purchase in question this indicates an equivalence, a substitution."[1]

Redemption was the means of our salvation. A price, therefore, had to be paid and an exchange had to be made: our lives for His life. But though the Innocent took the place of the guilty, by that very act it restored both the guilty and the Innocent. It laid a path and planted the seed of hope for new life here on earth, and eternal fellowship in the life to come.

Slaves Set Free

Once we understand redemption as freedom from enslavement to sin through external intervention, we must acknowledge that the sin that binds humanity is stronger than humanity itself. What, then, is its nature that it can hold humanity captive?

Sin is the agency of enslavement and death for all outside of Christ. Romans 5:21 portrays it as a reigning power exercising dominion over all of Adam's descendants. In tracing the historic roots of sin's tyrannical rule, Paul links sin's power to death, saying: "Sin entered the world through one man, and death through sin, and in this way death came to all people, because all sinned" (Rom. 5:12, NIV). The enslaving power of sin is all too real, devastating and ruining the lives of those held captive by it. A source of constant struggle, it is, by far, the greatest foe that humanity will ever face. It imposes its enslaving influence both from without and from within, leaving sinners desperate and helpless. Although they see the need for recovery, they are unable to obtain it on their own.

But hope does exist for the sinner. Just as the ancients often transferred slaves from one master to another, the sinner may exchange the mastery of sin for that of Christ. In Romans 6 Paul describes the shift of ownership of the sinner's life as the death, in baptism, to the body of sin and the resurrection to the lordship of Christ. Uniting with Jesus "frees" the sinner from the tyranny and *power of sin* (verses 6, 7). Death, the product of sin, no longer "rules" over Christ (verse 9). Therefore those who are in Him are no longer governed by sin or its by-product, death (verse 14).

Principalities and Powers

Sin, personified in Romans 5:21 as a power presently reigning in the world and exercising dominion over all Adam's descendants, exerts its influence over all those not in Christ. First John 5:19 declares that the whole world (referring to created life on earth) lies in a passive state, temporarily in the grip of an entity called the evil one.

Paul speaks in Romans 8:38 of *archai* (translated as "principalities," which could refer to civil rulers as well as to supernatural powers) that attempt to subjugate humanity. Another Greek word used in conjunction with the word "principalities" is *stoicheia*, which literally means "elements," or "elementary substances or principle." Paul therefore identifies a fundamental principle, or power, that rules the world.

The context in which he employs *stoicheia* reveals still another dimension of the nature of the fallen world and the powers operating behind the scenes. That aspect seems to connect spiritual beings to general forces or powers that control human life. Such forces, operating outside of Christ, may be political or social, and they may invoke the use of traditions and religious practices. Whatever the medium, whether it involves pagan rituals, the misuse of aspects of the ancient Jewish legal system, or the invention and dissemination of worldly philosophical principles, such *stoicheia* emanate from a common, dark parentage.

Of course, our twenty-first-century scientifically oriented society regards the concept of evil forces and demonic powers controlling the world as a holdover from an age of superstition and ignorance. As John Hicks observes: "Today we are more inclined, without necessarily discounting the possibility of evil spiritual beings, to reinterpret in terms of psychological forces most of the events that former ages attributed to the work of devils. The demons that tempt us or confuse us or lure us into evil are complexes and psychoses and libidinous pressures and the like in our own minds."[2]

In contrast, the Bible presents, as part of the reality of our world, an array of hostile forces comprising demonic principalities and powers. Though the biblical worldview incorporates naturalistic and scientific concepts, it certainly doesn't limit all reality to them. Scripture's perspective is large enough to encompass both the natural and the supernatural. But it serves Satan's purposes best when people deny his personal existence. As Ellen White insightfully notes: "None are in greater danger from the influence of evil spirits than those who, notwithstanding the direct and ample testimony of the Scriptures, deny the existence and agency of the devil and his angels. So long as we are ignorant of their wiles, they have almost inconceivable advantage; many give heed to their suggestions while they suppose themselves to be following the dictates of their own wisdom. This is why, as we approach the close of time, when Satan is to work with greatest power to deceive and destroy, he spreads everywhere the belief that he does not exist. It is his policy to conceal himself and his manner of working."[3]

The Bible teaches us that a series of powers, both personal and impersonal, rule our lives. Without Christ we are at their mercy, in whatever form they come. The pressures of the present moment; the fear of the future; and the demands of life, society, tradition, and ideology can all exert influences that can separate a person from the Lord. But Scripture also clearly teaches that Christ died to destroy "him who has the power of death, that is, the devil" (Heb. 2:14, RSV). Christ came to destroy the works of the devil (1 John 3:8) and did so at the cross.

If Christ has been victorious over the devil and over principalities and powers, why do we still wrestle with them? Why is the devil still able to roam about like a lion looking for prey to devour? Colossians 2:15, in which Paul uses three different verbs to describe what happened at the cross, may provide the key to answer this difficult question. The first is the Greek word *apekduomai,* which literally means "to strip off one's clothes." Here it may mean that the powers were stripped of their weapon. But what weapon? Consider the following: "Christ's life of victory, culminating in Calvary, spelled the doom of the devil. Satan's disguise was torn away. His methods of operation were laid open before the angels and the entire heavenly universe. He had exposed his true colors. By His cross Jesus Christ stripped from the principalities and powers of darkness both their robe of office and authority as princes of this world, and their armor of strength in their warfare against right."[4] While the cross did not literally destroy the devil, it did expose his weapons and methods of operation, thus weakening his effectiveness.

Paul uses a second verb, *deigmatizo,* which could simply mean to "publicize." The same word appears in Matthew 1:19, and in view of that text, the public exposure contains an added element of shame or disgrace. Together with the idea of stripping off one's clothes (noted above), the picture that emerges is of an intensified public display of shame. Again, while not signifying the devil's literal destruction, the cross publicly revealed the ignominy and shamefulness of his work. Having been thus publicly exposed, it undermined his power.

The apostle's final Greek word is *thriambeuo,* which implies celebration. The picture the verse paints is of the defeated, exposed principalities being drawn along in God's procession of victory, though the emphasis is on the celebration of a victory won, rather than the triumphing over an enemy vanquished. P. T. O'Brien rightfully notes that "these authorities are not depicted as gladly surrendering but as submitting against their wills to a power they cannot resist.... They continue to exist, opposed to man and his interests (Rom. 8:38, 39). But they cannot finally harm the person who is in Christ, and their ultimate overthrow, although in the future, is sure and certain (1 Cor. 15:24-28)."[5]

Yet what a strange and mysterious victory it is. Instead of legions of soldiers, mighty weapons, and waving banners, the symbol of victory is death. As Christ breathed His last, His end seemed to signal a terrible defeat. But the Bible calls it a triumph. The cross guarantees a complete and definite end to the evil that dominates our world. When that day comes, Christ will have dethroned every rule and authority and power (1 Cor. 15:24), and the last enemy to be destroyed will be death (1 Cor. 15:26). Until then, we must persevere and fight the fight of faith in the strength of God, knowing that Christ's sacrifice has already delivered a devastating blow to the powers of evil, and that the final battle for the souls of humanity is under way: "Satan saw that his disguise was torn away. His administration was laid open before the unfallen angels and before the heavenly universe. He had revealed himself as a murderer. By shedding the blood of the Son of God, he had uprooted himself from the sympathies of the heavenly beings. Henceforth his work was restricted. Whatever attitude he might assume, he could no longer await the angels as they came from the heavenly courts, and before them accuse Christ's brethren of being clothed with the garments of blackness and the defilement of sin. The last link of sympathy between Satan and the heavenly world was broken.

"Yet Satan was not then destroyed. The angels did not even then understand all that was involved in the great controversy. The principles at stake were to be more fully revealed. And for the sake of man, Satan's existence must be continued. Man as well as angels must see the contrast between the Prince of light and the prince of darkness. He must choose whom he will serve"[6]

---

[1] Leon Morris, *The Apostolic Preaching of the Cross* (Grand Rapids: Eerdmans Pub. Co., 1965), p. 61.

[2] John Hicks, *Evil and the God of Love* (San Francisco: Harper and Row, 1977), p. 209.

[3] E. G. White, *The Great Controversy,* p. 516.

[4] *The Seventh-day Adventist Bible Commentary* (Washington, D.C.: Review and Herald Pub. Assn., 1953-1957), vol. 7, p. 205.

[5] P. T. O'Brien, *Colossians, Philemon,* Word Biblical Commentary (Waco, Tex.: Word Books, 1982), vol. 44, p. 129.

[6] Ellen G. White, *The Desire of Ages* (Mountain View, Calif.: Pacific Press Pub. Assn., 1898), p. 761.

Chapter 6

Victory Over Evil Forces

Introduction

The opening lines of the eleventh Seventh-day Adventist fundamental belief read: "By His death on the cross Jesus triumphed over the forces of evil. He who subjugated the demonic spirits during His earthly ministry has broken their power and made certain their ultimate doom. Jesus' victory gives us victory over the evil forces that still seek to control us, as we walk with Him in peace, joy, and assurance of His love."[1]

Both Jesus' triumph and our victory over evil forces are part of the process of salvation. "Christ has indeed already won the victory over evil on the cross. Of that all believers can have the assurance. The history of Christian doctrine warrants us in saying that Christ's triumph over evil powers, into which victory the believer enters, is not only a victory *within* him . . . but it is also a victory won *for* him in a sphere outside and beyond his experience, yet essential for that divine redemption into which he has been initiated by faith."[2]

The real spiritual problem that some Christians face is that their walk focuses, not on attaining, through the power of Jesus, the certainty of victory over sin, but on using religion as an ointment to make life's daily challenges a little bit better. The Christian notion of salvation from sin grows foreign and gets replaced instead with the desire for salvation from life's headaches. Of course the Christian lifestyle has many practical advantages. But we must always remember that Christianity has an "otherworldly" outlook—a view of another dimension of reality beyond the material world. The overarching narrative of the great controversy between Christ and Satan needs to form the background for our understanding of the world and our place in it as Christians. In the midst of this conflict Christianity does not abandon its adherents to the mercy of the opposing forces. On the contrary, in Christ we have the promise of victory over them.

A Stage Set for Our Victory

We speak of *our* victory over evil forces, but in reality it is *Christ's* victory, and the Christian would be hopeless without it. Christ's death, by unmasking and disarming the forces of evil, has limited their effectiveness. That victory being established, our ultimate victory over evil became immanently possible.

In Ephesians 1:18-22 Paul prayed that the eyes of the Christians in Ephesus would be enlightened. The phrase "eyes of your understanding" (verse 18, NKJV), translated also as "eyes of your heart" (NIV), indicates a desire that the heart, the seat of thought and emotion, should receive insight. The apostle wanted the church in Ephesus to experience a new and deep spiritual awareness or illumination. It would fill the believers with Christian hope, give them an understanding of their privileges as God's heirs, and allow them to experience the power of God in their own lives. This great, immeasurable power, the product of God's mighty strength, and able to raise Jesus from the dead—would awaken new life and new understanding in all who took hold of it.

What Paul desired for the church in Ephesus is something that every believer may share. That experience is not the prerogative of a privileged few, but a reality into which all may enter. The incredible power that raised Jesus from the dead and now works in those who believe has also caused Christ to be raised above every principality and power, bringing everything under subjection to Him. The stage is truly set for the possibility of our individual victories over the forces that threaten to enslave us.

Hope of Victory

Christ's death and resurrection completed a past redemptive work and set the stage for the triumph of all believers. Our hope of victory now hinges on our willingness to engage, by the power of God, in a present work of submitting to Jesus and living a new life in Him (2 Tim. 1:1). The Bible teaches that all authority in heaven and on earth has been given to Christ (Matt. 28:18), and that all Christians who are *in Christ* also possess these spiritual blessings. According to Paul, it is because of God's work that Christians are "in Christ Jesus, whom God made our wisdom, our righteousness and sanctification and redemption" (1 Cor. 1:30, RSV). "God . . . has blessed us in the heavenly realms with every spiritual blessing in Christ" (Eph. 1:3, NIV).

The hope of new life in Christ is not mere theology—it is a reality that is the Christian's to live. The Christian enters the newness of the age to come and experiences, to some degree, the new powers of the kingdom of God. To be "in Christ" is to be in the realm of that new reality of life in Christ that He controls, and to live in genuine hope of victory. The foretaste of life in the new realm is to be the motivation for all Christian actions. Because of this, the Christian is encouraged to be strong (Eph. 6:10) and to stand firm (Phil. 4:1; 1 Thess. 3:8).

Christian hope is realistic. It avoids "presumption ('premature, self-willed anticipation of the fulfillment of what we hope for from God') or despair ('premature, arbitrary anticipation' of nonfulfillment, perhaps as resignation, 'humble acquiescence to the present')."[3] In Romans 8 we have a balanced presentation of the hope of Christian victory in Christ. Here Paul is under no illusion about the reality that faces the Christian. He recognizes present sufferings inevitable to the present evil age, the "between time" spanning the resurrection of Christ and the Second Advent. This period breeds tension and subjects the entire creation to frustration and futility (verse 20) as it anxiously awaits the coming of a new world order (verse 19). But Paul also understands that a new world order will arrive, and that our present suffering cannot be compared to the glory that will then be revealed (verse 18).

In Romans 8:26-30 the apostle gives at least two solid reasons for the Christian to hope confidently in the Lord. First, in our trials and "groanings" the Spirit *helps* us. The word translated "help" means to take part with, to assist in supporting, to lend a hand, to come to the aid of someone. It also connotes to shoulder or take upon one's self a great portion of a burden, responsibility, or task. The Holy Spirit comes to the aid of the believer. He shares the burden of the believer's trials and specifically intercedes for each individual according to the will of God. By the intercession of the Spirit all believers can know that their prayers are answered according to God's will, and that they do not shoulder their burdens alone. This is a reason to hope.

The second source of hope for the believer in Romans 8 is the knowledge that because of the agency of God, all things (suffering and tribulation in particular) work together for good (verse 28). But that is not because of some inherent potential in the nature of things. It is God's activity that brings out the positive outcome. Paul placed confidence in this promise because he knew that God's plans, laid from the very beginning for the sake of the believer, could not be frustrated. Having "predestined" (planned ahead) the salvation of those he "foreknew" (knew ahead of time), God would ensure that His plans would not fail (verses 29, 30).

The sacrifice of Jesus demonstrated, as nothing else could, that God's heart was tied to those of the faithful (verse 32). God is for us. And if He is, who can be against us (verse 31)? What can stand in His way? No entity or present circumstance or future event or power has the power to thwart God's determined plan to do us good (verses 38, 39). Therefore we can have confidence that He can use anything and everything to accomplish good in the lives of all who believe in Him. It may be that this good will be ultimately realized only at the end of time. Still, the fact that believers can know *now* that things will work out for good is a great source of hope and confidence in any difficult situation.

Christians Versus the Devil

Christ, having died for the salvation of humanity and setting the stage for victory, promises victory over evil to all who hide their lives in Him. James 4:7 is one of a series of admonitions that the apostle gives his hearers: "Submit therefore to God. Resist the devil and he will flee from you" (NASB). The apostle links submission to God with resisting the devil, recognizing that no one dares to do battle with the devil without first yielding to God.

Christians are not helpless victims at the mercy of the devil, but it is not their responsibility to confront the devil. God does that. James 4:6 tells us that God opposes the proud, and here the Greek word translated "oppose" is *antitassomai.* In verse 7 the word rendered "resist" is in the Greek *anthistemi,* which means "taking a stand against something." James's message is clear: what God requires of the believer is surrender and resistance. It is complete surrender to Jesus, who alone has power over the devil, which then produces within us the power to resist. When we in submission to God consciously resist the devil, he cannot fight back and must flee.

In 1 Peter 5:6-10 the apostle Peter, seeking to admonish a persecuted church, painted a picture of the nature of the conflict that engulfs the believer. Behind the suffering of the faithful was an archenemy, Satan, portrayed as a roaring lion seeking prey to destroy. The lion imagery sheds some light on why the devil brings suffering and persecution to Christians. Just as the lion roars to induce fear in its potential victim and thereby paralyze it, the devil tries to intimidate believers, hoping that at the prospect of suffering they might capitulate. But Peter admonished his readers first to be sober and alert and then, with firm *(stereoi)* determination, to resist *(anthistemi)* the devil. A cowardly attitude will not suffice. Taking a stand may produce suffering in the life of the believer for a little while. But God Himself will perfect, establish, strengthen, and settle the Christian who continues in faithfulness to Him (verse 10).

Examples of Victory

The Bible promises victory through Christ over evil. It is also full of real examples of such Christian victory. "The period of Christ's personal ministry among men was the time of greatest activity for the forces of the kingdom of darkness."[4] The great controversy entered a critical stage at that point in time. It was into this demon-saturated environment that Jesus sent out His disciples to minister. In Matthew 10:1-8 He instructed the twelve how to carry out their gospel commission. The right proclamation of the gospel would unmask the powers of evil. Therefore the disciples would go armed with power over demons and unclean spirits.

Two points are especially worth noting about this commission and the power that came with it. First, the healings and exorcisms were not to be an end in themselves. They were to *accompany* the proclamation of the gospel about the kingdom of God. As D. A. Hagner observes: "The four imperatives of [verse] 8 are *subordinate* to the proclamation of the kingdom. Healing of the sick, raising of the dead, cleansing of lepers . . . and casting out of demons are not of importance in themselves but only as a part of the good news of the kingdom—indeed, it is that which they exemplify and symbolize."[5] Leon Morris makes a similar observation by noting the lack of articles *(the or an)* to the imperatives (commands) of verse 8. Greek grammar employs the definite article to identify a class or group. Here in verse 8, the article is not connected to "sick" or "dead." Hence Morris observes that "most translations have 'the sick,' and perhaps this is the way we should take it. But since the word lacks the article, it may be that the direction is not that they should heal sick people as a class and thus turn into full-time healers. Rather, they were to preach the kingdom, and as an adjunct to that they were to do some works of healing. So, too, they were to *raise dead people.*"[6] "Again there is no article, so it is not the dead as a class that are in mind, but those dead people *whom they would encounter in the discharge of their commission.*"[7]

The second point of special interest is that the disciples were not to operate on a "fee for good news" basis. They were to make the gospel and the accompanying power freely available to all who desired it. The disciples were to treat others the way that God had dealt with them. Freely they received, freely they should give.

The sending of the 70 is our next example of victory over evil forces. The account is similar to the mission of the twelve, but different in some respects. Here Jesus did not specifically commission the 70 to cast out demons (Luke 10:9). Yet the 70 returned with joy, reporting that at the name of Jesus the demons were brought into subjection to them. But Jesus' response (verses 19, 20) places the matter of healing and exorcism in the right perspective: "Nothing less than the overthrow of Satan has occupied the Seventy(-two). Despite all the language of power inevitably involved in the description of this eschatological conflict, the ultimate issues of the kingdom of God are not power issues, but the sheer privilege of entry into the kingdom of God."[8] In other words, though the 70 disciples received power to subdue evil, they were not to rejoice in that power. Neither were they to make it their focus. From the perspective of salvation, the ability to control devils did not hold supreme importance. What had weight, what had value, what the disciples could greatly rejoice in, was that by the grace of God their names were written in the book of life.

In the book of Acts one story after another describes the victory of the believers over evil forces. We find the account of the healing of the man born crippled (Acts 3:1-11) and the reports of signs and wonders taking place among the people at the hands of the apostles (Acts 5:12-16). Then there is the curious story of a divining slave girl who repeatedly proclaimed that Paul and his companions were servants of the most high God who were proclaiming the way of salvation. Though seemingly harmless—even beneficial—a dark force lurked behind her shouts and actions. She was not talking about the true God, but most likely about a Canaanite deity also called Elyon (Most High). Paul, undeceived about the true nature of her cries, commanded in Jesus' name for the spirit that controlled her to depart. It left immediately (Acts 16:16-18). Authority and victory over evil were not restricted to Jesus and His immediate disciples. The gift of the Spirit (see John 14:16) gave believers the power to share Christ's victory in the cosmic conflict as they sought to fulfill the gospel commission. Believers are truly more than conquerors in the struggle with evil forces:

"The omnipotent power of the Holy Spirit is the defense of every contrite soul. Not one that in penitence and faith has claimed His protection will Christ permit to pass under the enemy's power. The Saviour is by the side of His tempted and tried ones. With Him there can be no such thing as failure, loss, impossibility, or defeat; we can do all things through Him who strengthens us. When temptations and trials come, do not wait to adjust all the difficulties, but look to Jesus, your helper.

"There are Christians who think and speak altogether too much about the power of Satan. They think of their adversary, they pray about him, they talk about him, and he looms up greater and greater in their imagination. It is true that Satan is a powerful being; but, thank God, we have a mighty Saviour, who cast out the evil one from heaven. Satan is pleased when we magnify his power. Why not talk of Jesus? Why not magnify His power and His love?"[9]

---

[1] *Seventh-day Adventists Believe . . .* , p. 149.

[2] H. D. McDonald, *The Atonement of the Death of Christ* (Grand Rapids: Baker Book House, 1985), p. 264.

[3] K. J. Vanhoozer, ed., *Dictionary for Theological Interpretation of the Bible,* p. 307.

[4] E. G. White, *The Desire of Ages,* p. 257.

[5] D. A. Hagner, *Matthew 1-13,* Word Biblical Commentary (Waco, Tex.: Word Books, 1993), vol. 33A, p. 271. (Italics supplied.)

[6] Leon Morris, *The Gospel According to Matthew* (Grand Rapids: W. B. Eerdmans, 1992), p. 246.

[7] *Ibid.* (Italics supplied.)

[8] J. Nolland, *Luke 9:21-18:34,* Word Biblical Commentary (Waco, Tex.: Word Books, 1993), vol. 35B, p. 562. Some manuscripts have the number of disciples sent as 72, although most have it as 70.

[9] E. G. White, *The Desire of Ages,* pp. 490-493.

Chapter 7

"Arming" for Victory

Introduction

Satan's ultimate goal is to wrest to himself the believer's allegiance to Christ. Before conversion, people belong to the devil. He rules over them. Although conversion to Christ takes the believer away from the devil's dominion, it does not completely shatter the devil's power. If anything, Satan increases his efforts to destroy our faith and win us back to himself. He employs his vast array of deceptive ploys, called "the wiles of the devil" (Eph. 6:11, NKJV) against us. Our only protection is to put on the whole armor of God.

This chapter focuses on how Christians can arm themselves against the devil's deceptions. Without God's armor we fall prey to the enemy. But with it, our victory is assured. We will therefore explore its nature and the protection it provides to believers.

The Need for Arming Personally

As Paul concludes his instructions about Christian households in Ephesians, he exhorts his readers, in view of the ongoing spiritual battle with forces of darkness (Eph. 6:11), to be strong in the Lord and in His mighty power (verse 10). In verse 12 Paul describes the Christian life as a struggle, a "wrestle" (KJV) against agencies of darkness. The word translated "wrestling," originally referring to hand-to-hand combat, implies an *individualized*, one-on-one struggle in which a person should be *personally* armed. The encounter is intense and violent, and Paul conveys this by describing the conflict in turn as a wrestling match fought in a gymnasium and as a battle waged on a battlefield. But one thing is certain—it is a conflict that should engage the attention of all true believers.

Paul exhorts believers to be "strong" (verse 10). But it is not an invitation to exercise willpower. Rather, it is an admonition in a passive sense that encourages the believer to "be made strong or strengthened." It is God's mighty power that fortifies the believer for the conflict. God invites every one of us to experience for ourselves His working on our behalf (see Eph. 1:19), power revealed as each of us puts on the divine armor. Paul therefore urges his readers to arm themselves individually (Eph. 6:13) to meet the conflict with success. God has made His armor available for our use, and we must equip ourselves with all of it. Nothing less than *all* will do.

The parable of the 10 virgins in Matthew 25:1-13, while coming from a different context, also speaks to the issue of personal engagement in spiritual matters. Ellen White applies the spiritual conditions of the five virgins to Paul's description of a class of end-time people who have a form of godliness but lack its power (2 Tim. 3:1-5). "This is the class that in time of peril are found crying, Peace and safety. They lull their hearts into security, and dream not of danger. When startled from their lethargy, they discern their destitution, and entreat others to supply their lack; but in spiritual things no man can make up another's deficiency."[1]

Girdle of Truth, Breastplate of Righteousness

"Stand therefore, having girded your waist with truth, having put on the breastplate of righteousness" (Eph. 6:14, NKJV).

The girdle, referring most likely to a leather apron that offered some protection for the lower abdomen, allowed freedom of movement to respond to any situation. In Luke 12:35, 37; 17:8 those who girded themselves placed themselves in readiness for service. The girdle was a basic, yet essential piece of armor.

The Christian's girdle in the spiritual battle against evil is truth. Lodged in the heart and free from hypocrisy, such truth fills the mind and heart with sincerity, wisdom, and discernment. It is by knowledge of the truth that the Christian is able to detect falsehood, the devil's weapon of choice. The Christian therefore dares not embark on the path of spiritual warfare without the knowledge and experience of truth.

Linked with the girdle of truth is the breastplate of righteousness. Viewed in the context of spiritual warfare and scriptural insights found in Isaiah 59:17 and 1 Thessalonians 5:8, it seems to involve moral issues. Doing right is as vital to the life of the Christian in the battle with the powers of evil as the breastplate is to the life of the soldier. Neglect by the Christian of his or her conviction concerning what is right leaves a gaping hole in the spiritual armor. But doing what is right and practicing righteousness involves taking on the righteousness of Christ. Devoutness, moral rectitude, and ethical behavior are meaningless if practiced apart from Christ's righteousness.

Gospel Preparation and the Shield of Faith

To facilitate movement over all kinds of roads, Roman soldiers often wore shoes studded with sharp nails. "One important reason for Julius Caesar's success as a general was the fact that his men wore military shoes that made it possible for them to cover long distances in such short periods that again and again the enemies were caught off guard, having deceived themselves into thinking that they still had plenty of time to prepare an adequate defense. In the victories won by Alexander the Great this same factor had played an important role."[2]

The armor is not yet complete, and Paul urges his readers next to put on the shield of faith (Eph. 6:16). The word translated "shield" comes from the word for "a door." The shield, measuring about four feet by two and a half feet and consisting of two layers of wood glued together, had the shape of a door. Because archers often dipped their arrows in pitch and then set them on fire, the wooden shield was covered with leather to extinguish the flaming arrows and blunt their tips.

The shield is prominent among all the weapons of defense. The spiritual analogy isn't hard to see. The "fiery arrows" of Satan are as wide-ranging as the wiles out of which they are devised. They arise from internal sources (lust, doubt, greed) or spring from external influences (persecution, tribulation, famine). "But faith in God, held aloft like a shield, catches them, snuffs out the flame, and makes them fall harmless to the ground."[3] Such faith goes beyond theoretical belief to belief in action. Not content to "believe" without doing, it actively puts up a defense against the assaults of the enemy. In the midst of the onslaught of evil forces, the active faith of the Christian takes hold of God's resources and extinguishes what the devil hurls. Of course, we can't save ourselves, and we can't fight the devil ourselves. Our battle is daily to choose the Lord and His ways over anything that the devil throws at us.

Helmet and Sword

The helmet of salvation as a metaphor most likely comes from Isaiah 59:17, though Paul applies it differently. In Isaiah 59 God wears the helmet of salvation, and in Ephesians the apostle calls upon the Christian to *receive it*.

Until now the picture painted of the donning of the armor is that of a soldier standing in battle array, having had his waist girded, his breastplate put on, his feet shod, and his shield secured. But something changes when Paul introduces the helmet and sword. He tells his readers to *take* the helmet. In doing this, he may be emphasizing the total "giftedness" of salvation. Salvation is not something that we can arrange to have but rather what we must accept from the hand of Another.

But in what sense can salvation be a weapon in the battle against the wiles of the devil? In 1 Thessalonians 5:8 Paul speaks of the helmet as the *hope* of salvation. But Ephesians 6:17 depicts the helmet simply as salvation, a reality that is at hand. Salvation in the New Testament is a present experience that will climax in eternity by deliverance from every kind of evil. The victorious helmet that God (Isa. 59:17) wears is now given to the believer as a protection. Because the ultimate goal of the devil's attack is to deprive Christians of their salvation in the Lord, the present assurance of salvation that is freely given to them becomes a powerful weapon to endure the conflict. In any spiritual contest the believer can truly proclaim with the psalmist, "O God the Lord, the strength of my salvation, You have covered my head in the day of battle" (Ps. 140:7, NKJV).

Some often argue that "the sword of the spirit"—the Word of God—represents the only offensive weapon in God's Ephesians 6 armory. While the sword is admittedly the most conspicuously offensive weapon, both in physical and spiritual combat, such a distinction is not entirely true. For example, the truth of God, by virtue of its sheer power to captivate the mind, can prove to be a weapon of aggression in the divine armory.

The phrase "sword of the Spirit" points to the role of the Spirit as the one who gives the sword its searing effectiveness. The temptation of Christ as recorded in Matthew 4:1-10 illustrates beautifully how the Word of God can be an effective weapon. Armed with the Word, Jesus was able to meet every temptation hurled at Him by Satan. Christ's victory through the power of the Word can be ours as well, if we choose to ground ourselves in the divine Word. "The reason why the youth, and even those of mature years, are so easily led into temptation and sin is that they do not study the word of God and meditate upon it as they should. The lack of firm, decided willpower, which is manifest in life and character, results from their neglect of the sacred instruction of God's word."[4] But when Christians buttress themselves with the knowledge, understanding, and experience of the Word of God, they are able to remain steadfast in the Lord.

Praying Always

Ephesians 6:18 begins with the phrase "praying always" (NKJV) and connects prayer with the donning of the armor. The putting on, taking up, and receiving of heaven's armor all require reliance on God. Hence, "prayer is not another weapon; rather, it is the spirit, the manner, in which the whole armor is to be worn and the battle fought. Paul is here urging a perpetual state of mind, a continuous attitude of communion with God."[5] The apostle stresses that in light of the ongoing spiritual battle, we must wrap every occasion in life in prayer. Such an attitude about prayer, while not always instinctive, is no less critical. When faced with problems, as helpful as it may be to consult friends and colleagues, prayer should always be the first line of defense.

Paul writes, "With all prayer and petition pray at all times in the Spirit, and with this in view, be on the alert with all perseverance and petition for all the saints" (verse 18, NASB). The phrase "with all prayer and petition pray" may be translated "praying with every kind of prayer and petition." Paul therefore emphasizes *variety* in prayer. Of the prayer that seems perpetually focused on asking for things, Ellen White writes, "There are selfish prayers, proceeding from a heart that is cherishing idols. . . . There are petulant, fretful prayers, murmuring because of the burdens and cares of life, instead of humbly seeking grace to lighten them. Those who offer such petitions are not abiding in Christ. They have not submitted their will to the will of God."[6] Not only cries for help but also confession of sin, profession of faith, adoration, thanksgiving, and intercession should characterize the believer's prayer life. Ephesians 6:18 emphasizes praying for others, which is fitting. As we pray for others, we ourselves are spiritually strengthened and better armed for the ensuing conflict, whatever form it takes.

Prayer must be done "in the Spirit," that is, the Holy Spirit and not the human spirit (see Rom. 8:15, 16). In the conflict with evil forces, the only prayer that will avail the believer is that made effective through the agency of the Holy Spirit. But praying in the Spirit involves more than calling on the Holy Spirit for help at prayer time. The reality we see in Ephesians is that "those who are united in their access to the Father through the Spirit (2:18), who are built into God's dwelling place in the Spirit (2:22), and who are being filled with the Spirit (5:18) can and should pray constantly in and through this Spirit."[7]

Finally, Ephesians 6:18, in calling for alertness or watchfulness, connects these two important concepts to prayer. When Jesus was in Gethsemane and found His disciples sleeping, He admonished them to watch and pray (Mark 14:38). Their safe passage through the crisis looming before them demanded prayerful alertness and watchfulness. Those who slumber at the approach of difficulty are caught unawares. But those who, with prayerful alertness, watch for the signs of distress are prepared to meet it.

---

[1] Ellen G. White, *Christ's Object Lessons* (Washington, D.C.: Review and Herald Pub. Assn., 1900), pp. 411, 412.

[2] W. Hendriksen and S. J. Kistemaker, *New Testament Commentary: Exposition of Ephesians* (Grand Rapids: Baker Book House, 2001), p. 277.

[3] *The Seventh-day Adventist Bible Commentary*, vol. 6, p. 1045.

[4] Ellen G. White, *Testimonies for the Church* (Mountain View, Calif.: Pacific Press Pub. Assn., 1948), vol. 8, p. 319.

[5] *The Seventh-day Adventist Bible Commentary*, vol. 6, p. 1046.

[6] Ellen G. White, *Our High Calling* (Washington, D.C.: Review and Herald Pub. Assn., 1961), p. 147.

[7] Andrew T. Lincoln, *Ephesians*, Word Biblical Commentary (Waco, Tex.: Word Books, 1990), vol. 42, p. 452.

Chapter 8

The Church: In Service to Humanity

Introduction

The church is an important player in the great controversy between God and Satan. But many today disparage its current state or dismiss its relevance, advocating "a churchless Christianity," a self-contradictory concept. Others rail against "organized religion," an attitude that is a far cry from bygone generations. In *The Institutes of the Christian Religion* John Calvin writes: "For such is the value which the Lord sets on the communion of his Church, that all who contumaciously alienate themselves from any Christian society, in which the true ministry of his word and sacraments is maintained, he regards as deserters of religion."[1] Strong words, but perhaps necessary counsel in view of the value the Bible places on the church.

The Bible teaches clearly that the church is vital. Not just an option, it's a crucial component in the plan of salvation. That is why it is central in the great controversy conflict and the particular focus of Satan's attacks. The church is a fundamental means to bring sinners into contact with God's offer of salvation. It is not a human invention, but "the house of God," even "the pillar and ground of truth" (1 Tim. 3:15, NKJV), a creation of God for the purpose of leading erring sinners into a saving relationship with Him.

Nature of the Church: Part 1

Today much literature and discussion on the church has a practical orientation—the church in relation to society, rather than the church as a phenomenon. On many issues people are no longer interested in knowing about the essence of things. Ours is a pragmatic culture, less concerned about "What is it?" and more focused on "What can it do for me?" To enquire about the church as an entity is to ask about its nature. When we speak about the nature of something, we are usually interested in its origins, function, and purpose. Without a proper understanding of the nature of the church, we risk imputing to it goals and purposes contrary to its essence.

The Bible uses much imagery and language to describe the church. One particular word, *ecclesia*, means "called out" or "called forth." In secular Greek life people used the word primarily for an assembly or gathering of citizens of a city summoned from their homes into a public place. For instance, in Acts 19:24-41 we find Paul and his companions in Ephesus in the middle of a riot involving the silversmith Demetrius. The Greek word translated "assembly" in verses 32, 39, and 41 is *ecclesia*. The Greek translation of the Old Testament (Septuagint) refers to the "congregation" of Israel, especially when it gathered for religious purposes, as *ecclesia*. The Jews were "called out" to be God's special people, and the early Christians may have used the word to identify those Jews and Gentiles who, as recipients of God's grace, had been summoned to be Christ's witnesses.

In the New Testament "church" describes the company of the faithful the world over. It never uses *ecclesia* with reference to a building in which public worship is conducted. Additionally, whereas the word "synagogue" originally indicated an assembly of people gathered for a specific purpose, the Christians preferred *ecclesia*. The emphasis is not on the place, but on the people. Both words indicate that the New Testament church was in historical continuity with the Old Testament church, the "congregation" of Israel (Acts 7:38).

Paul employs *ecclesia* to depict the church at three different levels: (1) the church in individual homes (Rom. 16:5; 1 Cor. 16:19); (2) the church in specific cities (1 Cor. 1:2; Gal. 1:2); and (3) the church in larger geographical areas (Acts 9:31). Since *ecclesia* represents any group gathered together in a saving relationship with Christ, Paul conveys the concept that each individual congregation is a representation of the whole church, not just a part of it. The whole is not greater than the sum of its parts—rather, each unit represents the whole. Understood this way, each individual, local, and geographical manifestation of the church bears great responsibility to illustrate the body of believers and the Lord of the church with fidelity and truthfulness.

Nature of the Church: Part 2

The word *ecclesia* helps us to see the nature of the church as a unique assembly of people called out to be witnesses of Christ. The New Testament also uses a wide range of imagery to describe the nature of the church, particularly in its relationship to God. Some have suggested that it has more than 100 such images, but we cannot discuss them all here. The three we will focus on are significant and allude to the Trinity: the church as the people of *God*, the church as the body of *Christ*, and the church as the temple of the *Holy Spirit*.

The People of God—Several passages in the New Testament present the believers in Christ as the people of God.[2] From these passages we can glean the following important points:

• Like the nation of Israel, the church is a well-identified group (Gal 6:16).

• The concept of the people of God emphasizes His initiative in choosing them.

• The concept stresses the element of belonging: the church belongs to God and God belongs to the church. God therefore cares and protects and provides for the church.

• The concept includes an expectation of unreserved loyalty: the people of God are marked with His exclusive claim.

• There is an expected holiness of the people of God (Eph. 5:25-27).

Two additional passages are worth mentioning. In 2 Corinthians 6:14 and following, Paul admonishes the believers to preserve their identity and integrity as Christians, writing, "As God has said: 'I will dwell in them and walk among them. I will be their God, and they shall be My people'" (verse 16, NKJV). Significantly, even as the New Testament applies the concept of God's people to Christian believers, it still uses it to describe the nation of Israel (Luke 1:68; Rom. 11:1, 2). And in 1 Peter 2:9 Peter describes the believers in Christ as a "chosen race," even a "royal priesthood," terminology that hearkens back to the nation of Israel. It seems then that in applying Old Testament descriptions of God's assembled people in a New Testament context, the Bible writers make a purposeful connection between the two. One is the continuation, and the consummation, of the other.

The Body of Christ—Several New Testament passages portray the church as the body of Christ. In Romans 12:5 Paul observes that "we, being many, are one body in Christ, and individually members of one another" (NKJV). First Corinthians 12:27 describes believers as "the body of Christ, and members individually" (NKJV). And in Ephesians 1:22, 23 Paul says, "And He put all things under His feet, and gave Him to be head over all things to the church, which is His body, the fullness of Him who fills all in all" (NKJV).

These texts, in combination with other passages throughout the New Testament, make the following observations about the nature of the church as the body of Christ:

• The church and Christ are united (1 Cor. 1:13).

• The church operates as the "hands and feet" of Christ.

• Christ is the sole source of nourishment for the church (John 15).

• The members of the church are interconnected. If one suffers, the whole suffers. There is therefore a need for genuine community and fellowship among all who belong to the church (1 Cor. 12:26).

• The church is universal with no distinction among members (Col. 3:11).

Temple of the Holy Spirit—Our final metaphor for the church is that of it as the temple of the Holy Spirit. The word *oikos*, meaning "house," nearly always appears in the Greek translation of the Old Testament and in secular

Greek in connection with God's name. When employed that way, it refers to a temple or a sanctuary. But in the New Testament the connection between *oikos* and God "is transferred from the temple to the congregation worshipping there."[3] When the New Testament writers began to conceive of themselves as the true Israel, they regarded their community as the New Jerusalem (Heb. 12:22). It was common knowledge that it was the Temple in Jerusalem that made the city the Holy City. But now the Christians did not feel constrained to think in visible, structural terms. God had erected His *people* as the temple to dwell in (2 Cor. 6:16). All the believers—whether individuals (1 Cor. 6:19), the local congregations (1 Cor. 3:16, 17), or the worldwide body of faith—together comprised the temple and dwelling place of God.

The metaphor of the church as God's dwelling place through the Holy Spirit has important implications. 1. Without the Holy Spirit in the church, it has no life or power. This life is expressed as the fruit of the Spirit (Gal. 5:22, 23). 2. Since the Holy Spirit is one, the church's unity evidences His presence (Acts 4:31, 32). 3. The church in which the Holy Spirit abides should be sensitized to His leading, remembering that it is the Spirit who guides the church into all truth (John 16:13; Acts 10:11-13) and empowers it to exist in holiness and purity.

The Mission of the Church

The church, as the body of Christ and an assembly of believers, has been established to do what Christ would do if He were still on the earth "bodily." Thus it does not simply have a mission—it is a mission. In Matthew 28:19, 20 the church receives an evangelistic mission to send out people to speak for God. God Himself undertook this mission in His work with the people of Israel (Jer. 7:25) and with the church (Gal. 4:4; Luke 9:1, 2; 10:1, 9). Jesus sent out His disciples just as the Father had sent Him (John 20:21). The church today can do no less. To remain faithful to its call, it must take up God's mission.

Besides to fulfill its evangelistic mission, the church also exists to edify its members and deal with matters of social concern. Such edification focuses on believers and involves building up their faith through teaching, preaching, and the use of their spiritual gifts (Eph. 4:11, 12; 1 Cor. 12:26; 14:12, 17, 26). Social involvement tackles issues concerning the health (Luke 10:25-37) and welfare (James 1:27; 2:1-11; 1 John 3:17, 18) of the community. It also speaks up to condemn social ills in any form, including racism and abortion.

Furthermore, the church has the responsibility to promote the true worship of God. The call to "fear God . . . and worship him that made heaven, and earth, and the sea, and the fountains of waters" (Rev. 14:7, KJV) is central to the great controversy conflict and will become all the more critical as it draws to a close. Revelation 14:7 gives a hint about the nature and motivation for true worship. Worship is not something we do at church to make us feel good. It is the reverence and adoration that we give to God because He is our

Creator (Ps. 95:1-7). Furthermore, it also stems from a sense of gratitude for redemption through the blood of Christ (Rev. 5:8-10). Because the "remnant" body of believers will reflect this type of worship, focused on God as our Creator and Redeemer, it will therefore be the subject of Satan's special hostility at the end of time.

Biblically the "remnant" is a nucleus of people who provide for a community's continued existence in the face of extinction. In the Old Testament it could be a physical or "historical" remnant, the last surviving people after war or natural disaster, or a spiritual or "faithful" remnant, the last remaining faithful who abide by the Lord's covenant. Revelation 12:17 describes a "faithful" remnant that appears at a time of spiritual catastrophe. Preserved by God at the close of the great controversy, this remnant honors God's commandments and has the faith of Jesus. It is an "eschatological remnant" entrusted with a unique mission: to proclaim to the world the nature of true worship and the need for fidelity to God's commandments through the preaching of the three angels' messages in Revelation 14. The Adventist movement identifies with the end-time remnant.

The church faces many challenges, but one of the most difficult is to keep a proper balance in its understanding of its mission. It is easy to get caught up in social reform and in working for the betterment of society. While that is important, we must never allow it to swallow up the ultimate mission of the church, which is to reach the lost for Jesus and to prepare people for His return. Evangelism is at the heart of the church's mission, and for Adventists the proclamation of the three angels' messages of Revelation 14 is critical to evangelism. At the same time, we must avoid the extreme of living as if every headline signaled the end of the world and thereby neglecting the basic responsibilities of daily life. We need divine wisdom to know how to strike the right balance.

Unity of the Church

The church, depicted as the "called out" of God, the "people of God," the "body of Christ," and the "temple of the Holy Spirit," is fitted for mission-oriented service. Unity is therefore essential, because without it the church cannot successfully accomplish its mission. This is why the issue of unity was on Christ's mind toward the close of His earthly life (John 17:21, 22).

Jesus prayed for the unity of the church (John 17:21, 22), and Paul exhorted the believers to be of the same mind and in one voice to give glory to God (Rom. 15:5, 6). But unending divisions have plagued the church. Revivals and concerns for world evangelization in Europe and America during the nineteenth century saw the birth of organizations such as YMCA/YWCA and the World Evangelical Alliance. Out of these movements and several conferences the World Council of Churches emerged during the second quarter of the twentieth century to help foster Christian unity.

Various groups have put forth differing expressions of unity. Some are satisfied with a unity of mutual recognition and fellowship. Others, seeking a more visible demonstration of unity, advocate a joining together of different denominations under a single banner. But the unity that Christ prayed for and that Paul exhorted the believers to attain involves a union of feeling, thought, and action. It is not a harmony achieved through social engineering, diplomatic management, or political subterfuge. Rather, it is a gift bestowed to believers by the indwelling Christ (John 17:22, 23) and maintained by the power of God the Father (John 17:11).

Several issues of theological and organizational nature seem to make the goal of uniting Christian churches a difficult if not undesirable proposition. Seventh-day Adventists hold conversations with other Christian groups and participate in ecumenical agencies as observers. However, given the sense they have of themselves as a prophetic movement, and out of concern for the integrity of the truth that God has committed to them to give to the world, they have formally declined to join organized ecumenical movements. But we should not regard such a position as a sign of arrogance or triumphalism. Rather, it is an expression of the church's commitment to positioning itself to fulfill the role of the end-time remnant, in drawing Christendom's attention to pertinent biblical truths.

Governance of the Church

The church cannot carry out its function unless it has in place a system of administration. Governance allows organizations to get things done and applies not only to general social life but also church life. It facilitates their arrangement into functioning, coherent entities with rules, regulations, and structures, thus permitting them to accomplish their intended tasks.

Authority is critical to governance and requires careful attention as to how it will be organized and carried out. Some churches, such as the Roman Catholic Church, follow an episcopal system of church governance in which authority resides with the bishop. Presbyterians have a system of governance in which, although the elder is the key officer, emphasis is placed on a series of representative bodies, with deliberate coordination between laity and clergy. Groups such as Baptists have a congregational form of church governance that stresses the role of the individual and makes the congregation the seat of authority.

Seventh-day Adventists have a representative system of church governance that incorporates elements from both the congregational and presbyterian forms. Ideally the leadership acts only as representatives, receiving delegated authority and responsibilities from the membership.

It is easy to point to certain similarities in structure between the Adventist system of governance and the one shown in the early church in the Bible and declare that our structure is therefore scripturally based. But a mimicking of certain features of Bible structure is not the goal. Rather, church governance must demonstrate sensitivity to biblical values that should underpin every action taken.

The first of these values realizes that the ultimate purpose of the church is to promote its mission of evangelism. In a number of passages in the book of Acts that depict the organizing of the people, the assigning of leadership, and the delegating of authority, these steps were taken for the purpose of advancing the gospel (see Acts 1:15-26; 6:1-4; 14:23; 15:1-29). A system of church governance that fails to meet this fundamental purpose is useless.

Second, although Christ exercises His authority through His church and its appointed officials, He never hands over His power to them. He retains the headship of the church (Eph. 1:22). The early church was conscious of the fact that they could not exercise any authority independent of Christ and His Word. Acts 15:28 emphasizes that it was important to the assembly that what they decided "seemed good to the Holy Spirit" (NKJV), the true representative of Christ. Holders of offices in the church today cannot act differently.

Third, in view of Matthew 20:24-28 and 23:8, those who exercise authority must remember that they are servants among equals. Whether clergy or laity, we are all of the same priesthood of believers (1 Peter 2:5), equal before God and united in our purpose to serve Christ and the church that He has established. At the same time, our recognized common priesthood does not give us unbridled independence to do as we like. Within that priesthood is an array of different talents and functions, and each must serve as they are called, performing the function for which they are best suited. As the various talents within the church unite in service to God, it strengthens the body of Christ.

---

[1] John Calvin, *The Institutes of the Christian Religion,* Book IV, Chap. X.

[2] The concept "people of God" also applied to the children of Israel (Deut. 14:2).

[3] Colin Brown, ed., *The New International Dictionary of New Testament Theology* (Grand Rapids: Zondervan Pub. House, 1986), vol. 2, p. 247.

Chapter 9

The Church:
Rites and Rituals

Introduction

Many societies and institutions in the world have initiation rites, sometimes called rites of passage. In most traditional African cultures such rites of passage help persons to transition from one stage of life to another. While they vary from place to place, they all have as their goal ensuring that younger members of the community will be productive community-oriented individuals. In the process, they take boys or girls as initiates, give them instructions on moral and social responsibility, and teach them the ways of adulthood.

A similar rite of passage marks a person's entrance into the body of faith. In participating in these activities, believers formalize their commitment to the faith and receive instruction and preparation on the principles and duties that guide the faith.

Naming the Sacred Rites: Nature and Function

Christians do not all agree on the names or terms used to describe the sacred rites, or even their number. During the early stages of the Christian church, believers in the Greek-speaking part of the church used the Greek word for "mystery" (*mysterion*) to describe Christian sacred rites. Where Latin predominated, the preferred term was "sacrament" (Latin, *sacramentum*).

A *sacramentum* was an oath a Roman soldier swore promising obedience to the commander's word. It therefore seemed a fitting description of the nature of the sacred rites. Through time, however, the word lost its original meaning and came to represent an *act* with an inward, invisible power. The church of the Middle Ages identified seven such acts, called "sacraments," that it saw as means by which grace was infused into a person's soul. Priests alone had the ability to dispense such power, and it could be given out without regard to the spiritual condition of either the participant or the priest. The seven sacraments recognized by the Roman Catholic Church today are baptism, confirmation, confession/penance, Eucharist, ordination/orders, marriage, and the anointing of the sick (last rites).

During the Reformation the sacraments came under scrutiny and criticism. In declaring their authority to dispense the power of the sacraments, the work of the priest had taken on a magical quality. Because of this, in the minds of many the word "sacrament" seemed tainted with misleading connotations, creating the need for a different term. The idea of "ordinance" replaced the concept of "sacrament."

The word "ordinance" comes from the verb "to ordain." An ordinance is therefore a special act that Christ Himself has instituted or ordained. To prefer "ordinance" to "sacrament" is to say that one participates in the acts because they are divinely ordained, and thus is a way for us to show our obedience and loyalty to Jesus as Lord. Passages such as Matthew 28:19, 20; John 13:14; and 1 Corinthians 11:23-26 confirm for Seventh-day Adventists that the foundation of our observance of these ordinances—the "why" behind what we do—is our desire to obey the Lord's commands. Understood this way, Adventists generally recognize only two ordinances, namely, baptism and the combined ordinance of humility and the Lord's Supper.

As mentioned previously, we observe the ordinances in obedience to the command of the Lord. But our observance goes beyond mechanical obedience. Each ordinance carries with it special symbolic significance. The importance of the ritual goes beyond the ritual itself and reminds the participant of vital spiritual truths. Prayerful observance of such rituals also promises spiritual blessings.

In spite of the importance placed on the ordinances, Adventists are united in the belief that they are not conduits of grace or acts to earn salvation or gain merit. Sin and its devastating effects are too serious a matter for rituals, even those instituted by Christ Himself. Only Jesus' death on the cross was sufficient to accomplish the salvation of deeply fallen humanity. To the degree that we understand ordinances as outward symbols of our union with Christ and our acceptance of His gift of salvation, they serve their purpose well. They are a means to an end, not an end in themselves.

Baptism

Most Christian churches practice the rite of baptism largely because in the New Testament it marks the beginning of the Christian life. The English word "baptism" comes from the Greek *baptizo*, which means "to dunk or immerse in water." The evangelical scholar Wayne Grudem writes that "the practice of baptism in the New Testament was carried out in one way: the person being baptized was *immersed* or put completely under the water and then brought back up again. Baptism *by immersion* is therefore the 'mode' of baptism or the way in which baptism was carried out in the New Testament."[1]

The New Testament uses several images to describe the act and its meaning. First, baptism symbolizes a spiritual union with Christ (Rom. 6:3-8). Through it, individuals participate in the suffering, death, and resurrection of Christ and renounce their former lifestyle. At the same time it links baptism with repentance and the forgiveness of sin (Acts 2:38), the new birth and reception of the Spirit (1 Cor. 12:13), and consequent entrance into the church (Acts 2:41, 47). Second, baptism symbolizes a covenant relationship with God through Christ (Col. 2:11, 12). It therefore represents, to a certain extent, what circumcision did in the Old Testament. Third, baptism symbolizes a transfer of loyalties from the world to Christ, and confirms the individual's consecration to Christ's service. The reception of the Spirit in baptism enables believers to serve the church and to work for the salvation of those outside the faith (Acts 1:5, 8).

As we understand the meaning of baptism, we see that its purpose becomes lost when used as a ritual for infants. As Acts 8:12 hints, baptism is meant for those who believe in the gospel message and are ready to commit themselves to it. Several years ago the Joint Committee of the Church of England on Baptism, Confirmation, and Holy Communion made an impressive admission when it stated that "the recipients of Baptism were normally adults and not infants; and it must be admitted that there is no conclusive evidence in the New Testament for the baptism of infants."[2]

Baptism requires faith, repentance, and the acceptance of a new life mission. Not only does it preclude the baptism of infants but also demands something more than blind, thoughtless acceptance by adult participants. Since God's Word produces faith and repentance (Rom. 10:17), it must therefore play a major role in the preparation of candidates for baptism. Having received spiritual instruction in the Word of God, candidates will be led to bring forth "fruits of repentance" (Luke 3:8) and to solidify their commitment to Christ through the rite of baptism.

Our understanding of baptism is shaped by our view of the ritual as a sacrament or an ordinance. Baptism, for those who view it as a sacrament, is the means that transforms a person from spiritual death to life. It is a supernatural event. Therefore age, spiritual maturity, and understanding and acceptance of biblical truth don't matter. But understood as an ordinance, however, the act of baptism is an indication and confirmation of an internal change that has already occurred in the life of the believer. It happened when the person accepted the Word of God, repented, and believed in Jesus and the power that He has to save. Baptism is therefore not appropriate to those who cannot, or will not, hear the Word, believe it, repent, and ask Jesus into their lives.

The Ordinance of Humility

Although only John (John 13:1-16) explicitly mentions foot washing as an ordinance, the rite clearly belongs to the ordinance of the Lord's Supper, which the Gospel of John shares with the other Gospels (see Matt. 26:17ff.; Mark 14:17ff.; and Luke 22:14ff.). For many Christian denominations it has become a forgotten or neglected ritual. But in John 13:14 Jesus highlights the moral obligation of His followers to follow the example of their Lord. "If I then, the Lord and the Teacher, washed your feet, you also ought to wash one another's feet" (NASB). The word translated "ought," and the tense in which it is expressed in Greek, depicts something that, out of necessity, should be done repeatedly.

The rite of foot washing demonstrates the meaning of true greatness in God's eyes. It was something that Jesus wanted His disciples to understand. So it must have been with immense pain that Jesus, faced with the cross, observed jealousy and infighting among His disciples and a jockeying for the privilege to be called the greatest in His kingdom. Their attitude showed that they had missed the point. To God, servanthood was the highest expression of greatness, and the ordinance of humiliation sought to convey that fact.

Jesus' exchange with Peter (John 13:5-10) reveals the spiritual importance of the rite of foot washing. The disciple initially understood Jesus' action in light of the traditional Jewish foot-washing ritual performed to honor guests. But Jesus' action had deliberate spiritual implications. He taught that a person who has received a full "bath," the symbol of baptism, does not need to repeat the rite (verse 10). But He also recognized that there is more to be done in the life of the believer and used the word "cleansing" (katharos), a word connected with the forgiveness of sin (1 John 1:7, 9). Even when we are born anew in the rite of baptism, in our walk with Jesus our feet sometimes slip and our path is sometimes sullied. The rite of foot washing therefore represents the cleansing, katharos, of postbaptismal sins. Jesus made it clear that if Peter refused His offer of spiritual cleansing—forgiveness of sin through the rite of foot washing—the disciple would have no part in Him. In this Jesus taught that those who refuse to engage in the rite of foot washing lose their spiritual inheritance (verse 8). But those who observe the ordinance experience the humility, spiritual cleansing, and fellowship the rite offers:

"The purpose of this ordinance is not merely the removal of dust from one's feet. This rite is a type of a higher cleansing of the heart, which is the source of alienation, jealousy, and pride. As believers stoop to wash each other's feet all thoughts of self-aggrandizement, pride, and selfishness are to give way to the spirit of love, humility, and fellowship. In this spirit one experiences union with God and with one another and is thus prepared to meet with the Lord in the celebration of His Supper."[3]

Before we go any further, we need to clear up a possible misunderstanding. If the ritual is not a means of salvation, why would refusal to engage in it cause a person to lose his or her "inheritance"? The rite itself has no power to save. Salvation comes from what Christ achieved for us on the cross. But the ritual is a sign of what the cross signifies. *Accompanied by faith*, observance of the rite testifies to the inward outworking of the reality that the rite represents. Refusing to engage in the rite, therefore, is an outward demonstration of what has *not* happened inwardly in the person's life.

The Lord's Supper

Baptism is the rite of initiation into the Christian church, and the Lord's Supper continues the spiritual experience that baptism began. Throughout Christendom the rite has received different names and varied meaning. As "Mass," prominent among Roman Catholics, the rite is a reenactment of the sacrifice of Christ in the present for the benefit of believers. Hence, though the bread and wine maintain their chemical composition as bread and wine, it is argued that they are changed *essentially* into the physical body and blood of Christ. As "Communion" (which in Adventism combines of the rite of foot washing and the Lord's Supper), the rite is a sharing in fellowship with Christ and one another. As "Eucharist," a word that means "to give thanks," the rite is a joyous celebration of what God has done through the life, death, and resurrection of Jesus Christ. Finally, as "Lord's Supper," it is a fellowship meal instituted by Christ as a memorial for believers of His death and second coming.

Matthew 26 offers an instructive description of the Lord's Supper: "While they were eating, Jesus took some bread, and after a blessing, He broke it and gave it to the disciples, and said, 'Take, eat; this is My body.' And when He had taken a cup and given thanks, He gave it to them, saying, 'Drink from it, all of you; for this is My blood of the covenant, which is poured out for many for forgiveness of sins'" (verses 26-28, NASB). The description draws parallels between the Lord's Supper and the Passover. The timing of the Lord's Supper coincided with the feast of Passover, and both have symbolic meaning. The children of Israel ate the original Passover meal in anticipation of the *salvation* that the Exodus from Egypt provided. When the Jewish people subsequently celebrated the feast of Passover, they did so looking back to that event. The original Lord's Supper was a foretaste of the *salvation* that the suffering of Christ would bring to all humanity. Subsequent celebrations of the Lord's Supper look back to Christ's passion and seek to bring its participants in touch with that experience. The parallel ends, however, when Christ takes the bread, breaks it, and says, "This is My body." In the Jewish Passover meal the broken bread represented the original bread of affliction, the unleavened bread consumed before the Exodus. Jesus now identified the bread with His body. By offering the bread to the disciples, Jesus symbolically assigned to them the benefits of His death.

When believers eat the bread and drink the wine, they dine with Christ in fellowship. Christ is present, not in the mystical transformation of the elements into His actual physical body and blood, but in the hearts and minds of all who are present and receptive to His leading. As Ellen White explains: "Christ by the Holy Spirit is there to set the seal to His own ordinance. He is there to convict and soften the heart. Not a look, not a thought of contrition, escapes His notice."[4] For Adventists, the benefit of the ordinance is not inherent in the material elements but in the personal presence of Christ through the Holy Spirit. The ordinance of the Lord's Supper speaks to our love for God and our gratitude for the broken body and spilled blood of Jesus. In imagination we join in the scene of the first Communion in the upper room, and thereby set forth Christ crucified among us.[5]

Anticipation of the Second Advent

The celebration of the Lord's Supper also points the believer forward to the second coming of Jesus, "when He had taken a cup and given thanks, He gave it to them, saying, 'Drink from it, all of you; for this is My blood of the covenant, which is poured out for many for forgiveness of sins. But I say to you, I will not drink of this fruit of the vine from now on until that day when I drink it new with you in My Father's kingdom'" (Matt. 26:28, 29, NASB).

In Bible times people often consummated a covenant—a solemn contractual arrangement—with a meal. They would, through eating together, commit themselves to fulfill their mutual obligations to the covenant. By sharing the cup and bread with His disciples, Jesus entered into a covenant with them, promising them that He would prepare a place for them and return to bring them home. No longer would Jesus partake of the fruit of the vine here on earth. But the promise was sure: He would drink it new with His children in the Father's kingdom (verse 29). So when we as believers participate in the Lord's Supper, we remember Jesus' covenant promise to come again. Until then, our duty is clear: "Do this, as often as you drink it, in remembrance of Me" (1 Cor. 11:25, NASB).

In a sense, the Lord's Supper spans the interval between Calvary and the Second Coming. Each time we share Communion we take our minds and our hearts to the cross and think about the great salvation that it has accomplished for us. But our salvation would be incomplete without the hope of the Second Coming. Christ's return will be the crowning moment of the plan of salvation. Until then, every celebration of Communion is an invitation to look ahead with great anticipation to the "marriage supper of the Lamb" (Rev. 19:9, NASB).

[1] W. A. Grudem, *Systematic Theology,* p. 967.

[2] *Baptism and Confirmation Today* (London: SCM, 1955), p. 34, quoted in M. Erickson, *Christian Theology,* p. 1102.

[3] *Handbook of SDA Theology,* p. 593.

[4] E. G. White, *The Desire of Ages,* p. 656.

[5] *Ibid.,* p. 660.

Chapter 10

The Law and the Gospel

Introduction

The previous nine chapters nearly all dealt with God's activities. They spring from His love for humanity and are the foundation of our hope and the good news of the gospel. The present chapter now discusses our response to God's actions. Salvation is ours to accept. Once claimed, it is also our privilege to grow in Christ and to accept the new responsibilities that salvation brings: "We are under a debt of gratitude to God for the revelation of His love in Christ Jesus; and as intelligent human agents, we are to reveal to the world the manner of character that will result from obedience to every specification of the law of God's government. . . . It is in this way alone that man may reveal the character of God in Christ to the world, and make manifest to men that happiness, peace, assurance, and grace come from obedience to the law of God."[1]

God's law—the perfect reflection of His character—is central to the great controversy conflict. It was a challenge to the law, and thereby to God's character, that introduced sin and set the struggle in motion. The conflict will therefore be finally resolved when sin is erased and God's law and God's character are vindicated. Meanwhile, the controversy rages on, and human beings must take a stand on one side or the other. Those who turn their backs on God choose sin, and follow the pattern of Satan by transgressing God's law and thereby attacking His character. But those who side with God choose redemption through Jesus Christ. They have died to the body of sin, and sin no longer has mastery over them. Instead, God empowers them to reflect His character in their own lives, thereby confirming the truth and beauty of God's law to the world.

God's Laws and Regulations

Because the Bible is a record of God's relationship with humans, it contains laws and regulations that are His instructions to His people. The Hebrew word *torah,* commonly used in the Old Testament, means "direction" or "guidance" and is often translated "law." The New Testament Greek translation of torah is *nomos,* "law." God Himself is good and righteous. Therefore His law is good and righteous and instructs His followers in goodness and righteousness. In other words, God's law reflects who He is. This is why we see in the Bible clear correspondence between the character and nature of God and the nature of the law. Just as God is perfect and pure, so is His law (Ps. 19:7, 8). Just as God is holy, just, and good, so His law is the same (Rom. 7:12). And just as God is true, everlasting, and righteous, so His law is one of truth, righteousness, and constancy (Ps. 119:151, 152, 172).

The Bible gives instructions governing many aspects of human life including health, sexuality, diet, work, and civic duties. Some of them are clearly universal in nature while others appear to be limited in time and scope. But all are God's instructions *(torah),* and we must use great care in developing principles to distinguish those that have universal application and those that do not.

Seventh-day Adventists and many other Christian groups generally make a distinction between "ceremonial" laws (regulations that taught the plan of salvation by symbols and cultic practices), "civil" laws (instructions regarding the community life of the nation of ancient Israel), and "moral" laws (instructions of God's pattern of conduct for humanity). The book of Leviticus contains a great deal of ceremonial laws, especially ones dealing with the sanctuary service and its ritual system. The nature of civil laws and the principle of justice underlying them appear, for example, in Exodus 23:1-9. The Ten Commandment law is the prime moral law in the Bible.

The Moral Law Today

Moral law focuses on right and wrong. The Ten Commandments are a concise declaration of God's will for right conduct as far as humans are concerned. Although the Decalogue (the Ten Commandments) was codified at Sinai, the book of Genesis suggests that human beings knew most of them before then (first and second—Gen. 35:1-4; third—Gen. 24:3; fourth—Gen. 2:3; sixth—Gen. 4:8-11; seventh—Gen. 39:7-9; eighth—Gen. 44:8; tenth—Gen. 12:18). Jesus looked positively on the Decalogue (Matt. 5:17), and the New Testament writers did the same (James 2:11; 1 John. 2:3, 4).

The Decalogue has biblical support for its universal application. 1. It is the only law proclaimed by God Himself (Ex. 20:18-20). 2. It was written to appeal to persons individually. 3. It is the only law inscribed on stone by God Himself (Ex. 31:18). 4. Its commands are in an imperative form, which seems to demand unconditional obedience. 5. It serves as the foundation to the other laws in the Bible. 6. It is the only law code in the Bible with a specific name ("ten words") (Ex. 34:28). 7. It was the only law placed inside the ark of the covenant (Deut. 10:5).

Most Christians today acknowledge that the Ten Commandments are God's universal moral code, and as such are still binding upon humanity. A number of legal battles have occurred in the United States concerning the right to have the Ten Commandments posted in public areas, including public schools and courtrooms. Other battles on other social issues invoke a concept of morality ripped straight from the pages of the Decalogue. Without question, in the minds of many, the Ten Commandments provide a valid standard of morality binding on society. But some argue that the Decalogue's time has ended, replaced by a new commandment.

Jesus said, "A new commandment I give to you, that you love one another; as I have loved you, that you also love one another" (John 13:34, NKJV). Did His "new command" upend the Decalogue? Not at all. It was, in fact, a neat summation of the Decalogue. In Matthew 22:37-40 He affirmed that love for God and for human beings, as stipulated in Deuteronomy 6:5 and Leviticus 19:18, was the basis of the law and the prophets. Greg Bahnsen, an ordained minister of the Presbyterian Church in the U.S.A., rightly observed that "we should not be misled into thinking that Scripture pits the summary or comprehensive commandments of God's law—i.e., to love God and one's neighbor (Lev. 19:19; Deut. 6:5; cf. Matt. 22:36-40)—against the law's specific details. The whole law in its various stipulations hangs on the two summary commands, but the summary does not abrogate or discount that which it summarizes."[2]

The Law and the Gospel

The debate about the continuing applicability of the Ten Commandments underpins a broader question: if we're not saved by keeping the law, what then is its purpose? Although the law and the gospel both have important places in the salvation of sinners, they often get pitted against each other. The gospel, it is said, speaks love, mercy, and forgiveness. The law, however, is rigid, demanding, and enslaving and focuses on punishment. But any perceived tension between the gospel and the law is just that—perceived. Understood biblically, the two concepts work hand in hand: "As Savior, Christ offers to mankind the gift of salvation and, as Lord, He calls for walking in newness of life (Rom. 6:4), manifesting the fruit of the Spirit (Gal. 5:22), and obedience to God's law (Rom. 8:4; Rev. 14:12) as the 'service and allegiance of love,' the 'true sign of discipleship' (E. G. White, *Steps to Christ*, p. 60)."[3]

In the Bible God's gift of salvation comes wrapped in covenants, and grace and law are both integral parts of His covenant. When Noah faced the Flood, God gave him a means of deliverance. Once that deliverance had been accomplished, God entered into a covenant with Noah and gave him instructions about how to live after the Flood (Gen. 6:18; 8:20-9:17). As God called Abraham out of his home country to a new land, He extended grace to him first (Gen. 12:1-3; 15:1-5), then ratified His covenant with him through a ritual (Gen. 15:18). And when the time came for God to deliver the children of Israel from slavery, He freed them from Egypt, then presented them the Decalogue as a means of preserving their personal freedom by following the directions of the One who gave them that freedom (Ex. 19:4, 5; 20:2). Such examples demonstrate a clear pattern: God extends grace first and then provides His instructions as the means by which a loving covenant relationship with Him can continue.

It is important to understand the proper role of the law in God's plan of salvation. Paul explains in the book of Romans that violation of the law as revealed in nature, in the conscience, and in the written Word of God, places humanity in a precarious situation. The human need, at that point, is justification before God. All attempts to regain favor or standing with Him through good works is therefore futile.

The deeds of the law could not justify, i.e., give "safe passage," to the presence of God, because the law existed only to provide the knowledge of sin (Rom. 3:20). The fact is that the law was never designed to be a means of salvation. By it, and through the working of the Holy Spirit, the law creates in sinners a recognition of their need for the grace (gospel) of Christ by reflecting to the sinner their true, fallen condition. As the evangelical theologian Walter Kaiser correctly observed: "To ask whether the law can bring salvation is to ask the wrong question as far as Scripture is concerned—in both the Old and New Testaments! Never does either Testament affirm, imply, or even hint that this might be the case. . . . It is a further error to argue that the writer of Hebrews (10:1-4) corrected the law, as if it had taught that 'the blood of bulls and goats [could] take away sins.'. . . The sacrifices were pictures, types, and models of the one perfect sacrifice that was to come."[4] The law points us to the necessity of the gospel—of grace. And this grace comes to us through Jesus. The function of the law, even in the Old Testament, was to show us our need of salvation. It was never a means of providing that salvation.

The Sabbath and the Law

As previously observed, many Christians still believe in the binding nature of the Ten Commandments. But the issue of the Christian's obligation to the law suddenly gets very murky when the question of obedience to the fourth commandment arises. The fourth commandment commands believers to *remember* the seventh-day Sabbath of the Lord God and *keep* it holy (Ex. 20:8-11). As part of the Decalogue, the Sabbath commandment carries with it the markers of universal application. It is a divine command written by the finger of God, and therefore places a responsibility on all believers to follow it.

Exodus 20:9, 10 explains the Sabbath commandment, carefully addressing *when* it should be observed (the seventh day), and the basis for its observance. The passage links the Sabbath to the biblical record of Creation week and makes creation the ultimate basis on which Adventists observe the seventh day. The seventh day is *the* day of rest that God chose at Creation, the day He designated for humanity to commune and fellowship with Him.

The absence of an explicit reference to observe the Sabbath as a commandment in the passage leads some to think that Genesis 2:1-3 does not prescribe adherence to the Sabbath. They argue that the Sabbath is a Jewish law later given to the Israelites through the covenant. Closer inspection shows, however, that the focus and reach of the Sabbath narrative in Genesis extends its application to humanity as a whole: God rested *in order to* be free for fellowship with human beings; God *blessed* the Sabbath, intending the bestowal of benefits toward those who keep it; God hallowed the *Sabbath*, the first thing He hallowed on the new earth, and thus gave the Sabbath the status of belonging to God.

When God presented the Sabbath commandment to Israel, He asked that they *remember* (Ex. 20:8-11). Remembering necessarily involves looking back to something that once was. Thus the Sabbath commandment was not a new invention but an invitation to look back to something that was possibly forgotten, and to reclaim for it the importance owed.

While many regard the observance of the Sabbath in the Old Testament as significant, they raise objections when we come to the New Testament. But the continued importance of the Sabbath in the New Testament is clear. Jesus was a Sabbathkeeper (Luke 4:16), and rejected only the Jewish body of laws, *halakah*, that sought to regulate Sabbath observance. The controversy between the Pharisees and Jesus concerned the nature of proper Sabbath observance, what "lawful" Sabbathkeeping looked like (see Luke 6:2, 9). Sabbath observance continued beyond Jesus, and Paul and his companions bore witness to its continued relevance and claim on believers (Acts 13:14, 42-44; 16:12, 13; 17:2; 18:4). As to the argument that the Sabbath shifted in the New Testament from the seventh day to the first, the following offers a concise answer: "There is no biblical evidence for Sabbatarianism that argues that the Sabbath rest has been transferred from the seventh day to Sunday. In the New Testament era, worship on Sunday was never described or understood as a Christian Sabbath. Additional complications are caused by Sabbatarians who argue that Christ brought an end to the 'existing Sabbath ceremonial' in Matthew 12:8. . . . There is in fact no Sabbath transfer or shift taught in Scripture. This constitutes a hermeneutical shift inasmuch as the meaning of the other nine commandments are not modified or qualified in this way in the New Testament. If the Decalogue is perpetually binding, including in the church age, how is it that this commandment can be eradicated or altered?"[5]

The Sabbath and the Gospel

Some have sought to link the Sabbath with Jewish law and thereby limit its importance post–Old Testament. One argument claims that Deuteronomy 5:12-15 is the first place that explicitly commands Sabbath observance upon the children of Israel. Given in conjunction with their Exodus from Egypt, the Sabbath is therefore a memorial of their redemption from Egypt. But as previously mentioned, the Sabbath has, from the very beginning, memorialized Creation (Ex. 20:8-11). Following Israel's deliverance from Egypt it also became a memorial of redemption and re-creation (Deut. 5:15). The Sabbath's subsequent use as a symbol of redemption did not override its foundational use as a sign of Creation. Creation and redemption belong together.

Others have taken Hebrews 4:1-11 as evidence that Christians no longer have any duty to observe the Sabbath, because those who have experienced salvation find their rest in Jesus. But by using Sabbath theology as an analogy to describe the rest in Christ, the biblical author in effect says, "Do you want to know what this 'rest' is like? It is just like the Sabbath." If the author chose to use the Sabbath as the main feature and reference point of the argument, then he must have placed great value and continuing significance on the Sabbath itself!

The author of Hebrews describes the Sabbath as the concluding event of Creation, God's rest from His creative work. Salvation is a process of re-creation, one that begins when we accept Jesus (see 2 Cor. 5:17; Gal. 6:15) and culminates in the re-creation of the heavens and the earth (see Isa. 65:17; Rev. 21:5). Sabbath celebrates Creation. Salvation celebrates re-creation. The passage in Hebrews therefore shows even more clearly the linkage of Creation and redemption. God has the power to make things new, a power celebrated in the Sabbath commandment. The commandment to remember the Sabbath is tied to God's act of creation (Ex. 20:11). The message of the gospel is that in Christ we are a new creation. When we celebrate the Sabbath, we remember the creative and re-creative work of God—in our world, in our lives, and in the new world to come. The Sabbath commandment therefore holds the promise of re-creation, and in that promise we find the law and the gospel bound together. Sabbath communion with God at Creation was a marvelous gift, but Sabbath communion in redemption is a gift even more marvelous.

---

[1] Ellen G. White, *God's Amazing Grace*, p. 58.

[2] Greg Bahnsen et al., *Five Views on Law and Gospel* (Grand Rapids: Zondervan, 1996), pp. 114, 115.

[3] Dederen, "Salvation," in *Seventh-day Adventist Handbook of Theology*, p. 307.

[4] In Bahnsen, pp. 394, 395.

[5] Bahnsen, pp. 81, 82.

Chapter 11

The Christian Life

Introduction

In the Bible, salvation does not concern itself solely with one's relationship to God but also the way we relate to each other: "If the world had before them the example that God demands those who believe in Him to set, they would work the works of Christ. . . . Our faith would be altogether different from faith now shown. It would be a faith that works by love to God and to our fellow men, and purifies the soul. If this faith were shown by God's people, many more would believe on Christ. A hallowed influence would be exerted by the benevolent actions of God's servants, and they would shine as lights in the world."[1] James speaks to the same issue when he asks, "What good is it, dear brothers and sisters, if you say you have faith but don't show it by your actions? Can that kind of faith save anyone?" (James 2:14, NLT).

The Bible emphasizes "sound doctrine" in the context of holy living (1 Tim. 1:10; Titus 2:1-5), pointing out that the true goal of biblical teaching is to produce a life lived to "love thy neighbor." The Christian is saved to serve as God's agent for the salvation and good of others. We are to be neither indifferent to the needs of others, nor so heavenly minded we are of no earthly good.

Stewardship

When we hear the word "stewardship," we sometimes, by default, think of tinkling coins, solemn deacons, and silver offering plates. But the concept of stewardship goes beyond money and holds deep theological significance to believers. Stewardship is "the responsibility of God's people for, and use of,

75

everything entrusted to them by God—life, physical being, time, talents and abilities, material possessions, opportunities to be of service to others, and their knowledge of truth."[2]

When Christians, through proper stewardship, use their time, abilities, and resources to serve others, they fulfill their God-given responsibilities and bring glory to Him. In hospitality (Rom. 15:7), in ministry (1 Peter 4:11), in keeping our bodies pure for God's service (1 Cor. 6:20; Phil. 1:20), even in simply living (1 Cor. 10:31), we give glory to God if we do all of these things for His sake. Here is the foundation of stewardship. Stewardship recognizes that the Lord has a claim to all that we have (Deut. 8:11-17; Ps. 24:1; 1 Cor. 6:19, 20; 1 John 3:16), and that He has entrusted us to care for them for His glory.

Christ purchased us for the sake of God's glory (Eph. 1:11-14). When sin entered the world, it diverted our purpose as conduits for God's glory. But God, through the plan of redemption, seeks to eradicate sin and restore the purpose that we lost when we fell. As we fulfill our mission as God's stewards, we evidence His work of redemption in our own lives. Our faithful execution of our duties brings Him glory and makes His goodness evident in His creation.

Tithe: A Mere Pittance

The ultimate service a Christian can render is that which helps to secure another's salvation in Christ. To further the ministry of the gospel, God "claims the tithe as His own, and it should ever be regarded as a sacred reserve."[3] The tithe is holy to God, set aside as sacred for particular use. We must place it in the context of God's redemptive work and appreciate it as a minor requirement in light of Christ's major sacrificial gift. Ellen White writes: "I speak of the tithing system, yet how meager it looks to my mind! How small the estimate! How vain the endeavor to measure with mathematical rules, time, money, and love against a love and sacrifice that is measureless and incomputable! Tithes for Christ! Oh, meager pittance, shameful recompense for that which cost so much! From the cross of Calvary, Christ calls for an unconditional surrender."[4] Yet the nature of our obligation to pay tithe remains, in the minds of some, a lingering unanswered question.

Almost all Christian groups teach some form of stewardship and acknowledge the necessity of supporting God's work. But whether such giving should be a tithe (one tenth of income) is not universally agreed upon. Most who dismiss the need to pay tithe argue that the "tithe" arrangement belonged to the Jews, who lived "under the law." But it is not an issue for those who view the law, not as a disconnected past reality, but as a present one that functions hand in hand with grace. They stress that the tithe, like the law, has continuing relevance and is an essential component to the plan of salvation.[5]

Nehemiah 10:38, 39; 12:44; and 13:5, 12 outline a system of collection for tithes and offerings on which the Adventist system is based. Those inside of Jerusalem brought their tithes and offerings to storerooms at the Temple (Neh. 10:37) while those away from Jerusalem went to collection points manned by appointed individuals. The tithe collected both inside and outside of Jerusalem went to the Levites (12:44) who then returned to the Temple a tithe on the amount they received (Neh. 10:38). The Levites then used the balance of the tithe for their personal support.

The Seventh-day Adventist Church takes several principles from these passages to effect an organized collection of the Lord's tithes: (1) a centralized collection and distribution of tithes; (2) the appointment of specific individuals to organize the collection and distribution; (3) the establishment of "outposts" at the local level to collect and distribute the tithe. Such procedures help ensure that the tithes are "brought into the treasury to be used in an orderly way to sustain the gospel laborers in their work."[6]

The Responsibility for One's Self

As redeemed believers and stewards of God, we have responsibilities to others. But we cannot carry them out if we behave irresponsibly toward ourselves. Believers united with Christ (Gal. 2:20) desire to live a life ordered after Christ's impulses. To live responsibly, we must live for Christ's sake (2 Cor. 5:14, 15; 1 Cor. 10:31). We must, by the power of God, have the mind of Christ within us (Phil. 2:5) and heed the call to holiness, separating ourselves from earthy passions and moral impurity (1 John 3:22; 1 Peter 1:14-16). The motivation to live for Christ must be present in every aspect of the Christian's life. For example, the Bible is concerned about how to preserve human health and provides guidelines on nutrition (Gen. 1:29, 30; Lev. 11:1-47; 17:10-15), rest (Gen. 2:2; Ex. 20:8-11), and stress (Matt. 6:25; Luke 12:22-29; 1 Peter 5:7). Certain stories and passages demonstrate the important place that health holds in Scripture (Dan. 1:11-16; 3 John 2). As a result, we stress the health benefits of exercise, sunlight, water, fresh air, good nutrition, and abstinence from drugs and stimulants, such as caffeine. But those who live with the mind of Christ understand that abstinence from injurious products is not the sum of our duties. Even in dealing with the good things of nature, we must use them wisely and judiciously.

The same care, guided by the mind of Christ and the desire to live life for His sake, colors other areas of life. In the way that we dress we follow principles of modesty and a desire to divert attention away from ourselves to Jesus. And in our choice of recreation we seek that which is wholesome and meaningful and avoid meaningless and purposeless leisure that can be an avenue of evil to the mind and heart. Thus whatever actions we take, words we speak, or attitudes we adopt, everything that we do must be all to the glory of God.

Christian Marriage

One of the basic social expressions of interhuman relationships is the institution of marriage. To understand the biblical concept of marriage, we need to go to the Creation story in Genesis. The Garden of Eden, Adam's first home, was the picture of perfect beauty and harmony. Yet for Adam, alone in the magnificent garden, something was missing. So from his own bone God fashioned the missing component, a helper and companion. And seeing her for the first time, Adam declared, "'This is now bone of my bones, and flesh of my flesh; she shall be called Woman, because she was taken out of Man.' For this reason a man shall leave his father and his mother, and be joined to his wife; and they shall become one flesh" (Gen. 2:23-25, NASB).[7]

Today people sometimes declare marriage incapable of definition since its meaning differs from one individual to another and from one time to another. In the Bible, however, the definition is clear. From the Creation narrative to passages throughout the Scriptures, the Bible understands marriage as an institution established by God, in which an adult man and adult woman covenant with each other to enter into an intimate and lasting personal relationship. Scripture depicts marriage as marked by an appreciation of the equality of male and female, a deep bond of unity and blended goals, and a sense of permanence and faithfulness.

Of course, as we know all too well, marriage, even within the church, too often gets treated with frivolity as people casually jump from one relationship to another. Society in general finds itself challenged by issues surrounding polygamy, divorce, remarriage, cohabitation, homosexuality, and same-sex marriage. Adultery, fornication, and pornography abound. Sexual perversions and irregularities, such as rape, incest, and child abuse, plague our communities. While society in general faces difficulty in grappling with such problems, the Bible has clear guidelines and counsel that we can bring to bear on them (see Matt. 5:32; 19:5-9; Mark 10:11, 12; Rom. 7:2, 3; 1 Cor. 7; Gen. 19:4-10 [cf. Jude 7, 8]; Rom. 1:26-28). Contemporary culture may equivocate on such matters, but they are serious human failings upon which God looks with compassion and tenderness and which He offers victory over through His grace. Therefore, rather than attempting to rationalize such problems away, we must reach for God's ideal and for the help He provides to attain it: redemption and salvation through Jesus.

Christian Behavior

Christians ought not to be of the world. But they must necessarily operate within it (John 17:14-18). Interaction with society is therefore a required and welcome component of the Christian's experience, and an opportunity to demonstrate divine love to the world. We must conduct such interaction with a view to bring glory to God and rightly to reflect His character. We will look at three areas of social interaction and consider the Christian's responsibilities within them: the employer/employee relationship, civic duties, and social responsibility.

The employer/employee relationship is ubiquitous in contemporary society, and the Bible has insights on the responsibilities of employers and employees alike. In James 5:4-6 the apostle speaks against injustice in the workplace, painting a picture in which the unpaid wages of wronged workers cry out against the defrauding employer. Christian employers must remember that their employees are their equals before Christ (Eph. 6:9). They must also be guided by the principle that adequate work requires adequate compensation.

On the employee side, Paul encourages workers to be "filled with conscientious solicitude when they recognize the real nature of their assignment, namely, so to conduct themselves toward their masters that the latter whether they be believers or not, will be able to see what the Christian faith accomplishes within the hearts of all who practice it."[8] In other words, Christian workers are ambassadors of Christ even in the workplace, and the nature and quality of their work will witness to their faith in Jesus. Christian workers must therefore resist the temptation to be slothful at duty, an attitude that first develops at home. "Parents cannot commit a greater sin than to allow their children to have nothing to do. The children soon learn to love idleness, and they grow up shiftless, useless men and women. When they are old enough to earn their living, and find employment, they work in a lazy, droning way, yet expect to be paid as much as if they were faithful."[9]

Christians also have civic duties to their communities (see Rom. 13:1-7) and a responsibility to speak out against social ills. Long ago Ellen White remarked that such social issues as slavery, unjust racial prejudices, and oppression of the poor are "a serious menace to the well-being of the human race, and as evils which the church of Christ is appointed by her Lord to overthrow."[10] More recently Jan Paulsen, former president of the worldwide Seventh-day Adventist Church, noted that "as a church—and individuals—we have not only the right, but the obligation, to be a moral voice in society; to speak clearly and eloquently on that which touches our core values. Human rights, religious freedom, public health, poverty, injustice—these are some of the areas in which we have a God-given responsibility to *advocate* for those who cannot speak for themselves."[11]

Christians make God's will the motivating factor behind all their actions. As Peter said in Acts 5:29, "We ought to obey God rather than men" (NKJV). But "loyalty to God first does not entitle anyone to become autonomous and create social disharmony or chaos. Christians pay taxes, participate in civic duties, respect traffic laws and property regulations, and cooperate with civil authorities in curbing or controlling crime and violence."[12] When Christians faithfully discharge the duties set on them by society, duties not otherwise contrary to the will of God, they honor Him and promote peace and responsibility in their community (see Rom. 13).

Finally, Christians must take seriously the challenge of social responsibility. God has commanded us to feed the hungry, give drink to the thirsty, and clothe the naked. Our commitment to such duties is the sign of our union with Christ. In fact, in His parable in Matthew 25:31-46 it was the standard by which He distinguished the saved from the lost.[13]

While social responsibility is not the total gospel commission, it is nevertheless a critical dimension that we cannot neglect. H. Richard Niebuhr correctly observed, "The Christian can exercise his calling to seek the kingdom of God if, motivated by love of neighbor, he carries on his work in the moral communities of family and economic, national, and political life. . . . Only by engaging in civic work for the sake of the common good, by faithfulness in one's social calling is it possible to be true to the example of Christ."[14]

---

[1] Ellen G. White, *Welfare Ministry* (Washington, D.C.: Review and Herald Pub. Assn., 1952), p. 297.

[2] *Seventh-day Adventist Encyclopedia* (Washington, D.C.: Review and Herald Pub. Assn., 1996), vol. 11, p. 705.

[3] E. G. White, *Christ's Object Lessons*, p. 300.

[4] E. G. White, *Testimonies to the Church*, vol. 4, pp. 119, 120.

[5] Actually, on the issue of tithing, we have at least one suggestion that the Old Testament system ought to be the model for the New Testament church (1 Cor. 9:13, 14). And we find specific lessons from the Old Testament system that we can apply to the church today.

[6] E. G. White, *Manuscript Releases,* vol. 19, p. 376.

[7] Other passages that speak to the nature of marriage include Malachi 2:14, Ephesians 5:28, and 1 Corinthians 7:4.

[8] W. Hendriksen and S. J. Kistemaker, *New Testament Commentary: Exposition of Ephesians,* pp. 263, 264. In Ephesians 6:5-8 Paul addresses the situation of the slave, in a limited way, the equivalent of today's employee. Far from endorsing slavery, Paul sought to overthrow it from within.

[9] E. G. White, *Christ Object Lessons*, p. 345.

[10] Ellen G. White, *Life Sketches of Ellen G. White* (Mountain View, Calif.: Pacific Press Pub. Assn., 1915), p. 473.

[11] Jan Paulsen, "Serving Our World, Serving Our Lord," *Adventist World,* May 2007. p. 9. (Italics supplied.)

[12] Miroslav M. Kis, in *Handbook of Seventh-day Adventist Theology*, p. 701.

[13] In both the Old and New Testaments we have passages that address this issue (see Lev. 25:25-55; Isa. 61:1-3).

[14] H. Richard Niebuhr, *Christ and Culture* (New York: Harper and Row, 1951), p. 97.

Chapter 12

Last Things:
Jesus and the Saved

Introduction

The cross was the climax of God's love, and since then His people have had a saving relationship with Him through the atoning death of Christ. Nevertheless, biblical prophecy points to a "time of the end" (Dan. 12:4, 9). It is a period in salvation history when Christ will have a special relationship with those who have found salvation in His atoning sacrifice. Three particular events within the "time of the end" have immense spiritual implications: Christ's ministry in the heavenly sanctuary, the second coming of Christ, and the resurrection.

The Heavenly Sanctuary

Hebrews 8:1, 2 depicts the heavenly sanctuary as a real place, yet the biblical idea of a sanctuary in heaven has struggled for acceptance. Greek Church Fathers, who came under the influence of Greek philosophical dualism, overlooked it, an attitude carried into the Middle Ages. However, the Reformation would correct that. Luther, Calvin, and the Puritans affirmed a literal heavenly sanctuary in which Jesus ministers. More recent times have treated the sanctuary as a metaphor or figure of speech for God's presence and not an actual physical place.

Adventists base their interest in the heavenly sanctuary on the earthly sanctuary, described as a type or pattern of the heavenly (Ex. 25:8, 9). If indeed the earthly sanctuary in Israel followed the pattern of the one in heaven, there is at least a functional correspondence between the two, and the earthly sanctuary reveals much about the heavenly. The ministrations of the earthly sanctuary offer us a window into the realities of the heavenly sanctuary and God's means of teaching His people the principles of salvation. The earthly sanctuary foreshadowed the "real thing," Christ's ministry in heaven (Heb. 9:9–15).

In the earthly sanctuary priests sacrificed animals and made atonement on a daily basis in the holy place (Lev. 4:6, 7) and annually in the Most Holy Place (Lev. 16). These basic activities point to three important truths about the process of salvation. First, the shedding of blood was, and is, necessary for atonement of sin (Heb. 9:22). Second, even with the shed blood and atonement, there was, and still is, the need for a priestly mediator between sinners and a holy God, and the blood was the enabling basis of such mediation. Third, the ministry of the priest in the Most Holy Place during the Day of Atonement cleansed the sanctuary of sin. But it required self-examination and an affliction of the soul on the part of the people during this solemn experience of judgment. By such affliction and repentance, however, the people would be saved within the assembly of God's people and not cut off from it.

Because of the finality of the cross event for the salvation of humanity, it is easy to conclude that everything about our salvation ended at the cross. But the Bible says that Christ went up to heaven (Acts 1:11) "to save forever those who draw near to God through Him, since He always lives to make intercession for them" (Heb. 7:25, NASB). The book of Hebrews is very helpful in clarifying the apparent conflict between the finality of the cross event and the continuing validity of Christ's ministry in the heavenly sanctuary. Hebrews 1:3 presents Jesus as Son, but from Hebrews 7:27 to 8:1 portrays Him as high priest. The book of Hebrews points out that the one known as God's Son is the same one to be recognized now as our high priest.

Just as the earthly sanctuary service revealed three phases of salvation—substitutionary sacrifice, priestly mediation, and judgment—the Bible teaches that all three are embodied in the ministry of Christ on behalf of sinners. Christ died as our substitute, the first phase of salvation. Isaiah 53 aptly describes His death in our place, especially verses 4-6. Both modern Jewish and many Christian Bible expositors, however, deny that the passage applies to the predicted Messiah or Christ. The Gospels, however, make a clear application of Isaiah 53 to Christ (Matt. 8:17; John 12:38). *The Seventh-day Adventist Bible Commentary* observes that "verses 4-6 [of Isaiah 53] emphasize the vicarious nature of Christ's sufferings and death. The fact that it was for us, and not for Himself, that He suffered and died is reiterated nine times in these verses, and again in verses 8, 11. He suffered in our stead. The pain, humiliation, and abuse that we deserve, He took upon Himself."[1] Ellen G. White concurs: "Christ was treated as we deserve, that we might be treated as He deserves. . . . He suffered the death which was ours, that we might receive the life which was His. 'With His stripes we are healed.' "[2]

Christ acts as our mediator. This second phase of salvation embodies the ministry of Christ as our priestly mediator. Just as animal sacrifices pointed to the death of Christ, the priestly ministry foreshadowed the true ministry of Christ in the heavenly sanctuary. In particular, the daily ministry of the earthly priests in the holy place symbolizes the access the sinner has to God through Christ's ministry as intercessor and mediator in the heavenly sanctuary (Heb. 4:14-16). Indeed, part of the main point that the book of Hebrews tries to make is precisely that Christ has a better priestly ministry than the Levitical priesthood. Christ's priesthood is not only the antitype of the Levitical order; it is of a better order (the order of Melchizedek, Heb. 7:11, 12, 18, 19; 8:13).[3]

Christ is our high priest. The third phase of salvation embodies the judgment and Christ's ministry in the heavenly sanctuary. Hebrews 9:23 is the key text to understanding it. The text points out that the earthly sanctuary and things pertaining to it are *the copies of the heavenly things*, and that both needed to be cleansed by sacrifice, though the heavenly things required a better sacrifice. Without question the word "cleansing" points to the ministry of the high priest in the Most Holy Place on the Day of Atonement. On that day the Lord judged Israel, not on how good they had managed to be, but on whether they had humbled themselves and accepted God's forgiveness and cleansing through the ministry of the high priest. Those who had not done so found themselves cut off from the people (Lev. 23:29). Christ performs this same ministry in the heavenly sanctuary on behalf of His people, and they too have the opportunity to accept what He freely offers.

The cleansings mentioned in Hebrews 9:23, connected as they are to the judgment phase of Christ's ministry, give us an idea about the timing of the cleansing event. Daniel 8:13, 14 contains the 2300-day prophecy and by its language connects that prophecy to the sanctuary service and the Day of Atonement. In Daniel 9 God sends the angel Gabriel to give Daniel understanding about the prophecy he received in chapter 8. The angel's answer, however, describes a 70-week prophecy and seems therefore to connect the 70 weeks to the 2300 days. The 70 weeks, or 490 years, are cut off from the larger 2300 days, or years, and both share the same starting point of 457 B.C., when Artaxerxes issued the critical decree to rebuild Jerusalem. Calculating from that time, we find that the 2300 years ended in A.D. 1844, the prophetic date for the cleansing of the sanctuary. That year marked a transition in the heavenly ministry of Jesus to the judgment phase of salvation. We are therefore living in the midst of a unique end-time experience with our intercessor and mediator, Jesus.

The Second Coming of Christ

In Acts 3:19-21 Peter brought his second sermon to a close by calling his Jewish audience to repentance. Such repentance would wipe out their sins and bring times of refreshing from the presence of the Lord. God would send Jesus, the Christ appointed for them. But when would those things happen? Was the wiping out of sins referring to a present reality or to the cleansing of sins at the end of time? The statement that Christ would be sent has also garnered discussion and elicited many different interpretations. "The question still remains," writes J. B. Polhill, "does 3:19-21 presuppose a Jewish messianic concept that understood the first coming of the Messiah as being predicated upon the repentance of Israel? The passage could surely be so viewed if taken in isolation from its context. In the context of Peter's sermon, however, something quite different is expressed."[4] Polhill continues, "The Messiah indeed has come as the glorified Servant, the Holy and Righteous One of God. But the Jerusalem Jews did not receive him as Messiah; they disowned him. He is indeed the Messiah appointed by God, but they failed to recognize and receive him as their Messiah. The Messiah will come again to restore his kingdom to Israel."[5]

We may fairly conclude that while Peter may not have known the "times or seasons" (Acts 1:7), his prior reference to Joel's prophecy in Acts 2:14-21 indicated an appreciation for the fulfillment of prophecy, even in his time. In his prophetic frame of mind "Peter, speaking by inspiration, and thus beyond his own finite understanding, is referring, tersely, to two great events of earth's last days—(1) the mighty outpouring of God's Spirit, and (2) the final blotting out of the sins of the righteous—which are tied to a third climactic event, the second advent of Christ."[6]

The early Christians treasured the promise of the second coming of Christ. The early church was certain of the second coming of Christ as the blessed hope, the promise of a new heaven and earth (2 Peter 3:13). Christ's first advent provided a theological rationale for His second. He had come, as promised, the first time. Now He was sure to appear, as promised, the second time. The eradication of the sin problem is consummated in the "cleansing of the sanctuary," His coming the "second time for salvation" (Heb. 9:26, 28). Christ's second advent is therefore really a dimension of the process of salvation. The return of Christ will mark the conclusion of the great controversy as far as humanity's destiny is concerned.

Satan, seeing the end of the struggle in sight and ever desperate to wrench souls to his side, will seek through deception to lead many astray. Ellen White tells us that "as the second appearing of our Lord Jesus Christ draws near, satanic agencies are moved from beneath. Satan will not only appear as a human being, but he will personate Jesus Christ, and the world that has rejected the truth will receive him as the Lord of lords and King of kings."[7] But Scripture has declared that Christ's return will be a literal, personal, visible, audible, and glorious cataclysmic event (Matt. 24:27; Acts 1:11; and 1 Thess. 4:16; 5:2, 3).

Awaiting the Advent

Among Christians, the thought of the nearness of the second coming of Christ evokes a spectrum of reactions from fear to joyful anticipation. Some Christians engage in unhelpful speculative activities, obsessively tying everyday events to signs of the Advent. Others dismiss evidences of the nearness of

Christ and live in self-inflicted oblivion about His soon return. True followers of Christ will be neither afraid of nor surprised by His second coming
(1 Thess. 5:1-6). Instead, they will examine and interpret signs carefully and
use them for their intended purpose—not to satisfy curiosity or excite anxiety
or fear, but to encourage believers to maintain an attitude of hope, confidence,
and watchfulness (Matt. 24:32-44; John 13:19; 14:29).

For the guidance and comfort of believers, the Bible predicts events in nature, the religious world, and the moral world that will mark the last days. A
decline in moral life similar to that found in the days of Noah and the days of
Lot in Sodom will sweep the world before the Second Coming (Luke 17:26-
28). The Bible also tells us that before Jesus' second advent earthquakes will
strike the earth and signs will appear in the sun and the moon. Because such
signs and events occur on a regular basis in different parts of the world, some
have discounted the relevance of the biblical predictions. But when Jesus made
them, He placed them in a specific time frame—just after a great tribulation
and just before His appearing (Mark 13:24-26; Matt. 24:29, 30). Adventists
understand the great tribulation as the 42 prophetic months of persecution described in Revelation 12:13-17 and 13:1-10. By prophetic reckoning, it began
in A. D. 538 and ended in 1798. Based on this reading the Lisbon earthquake
on November 1, 1755, the darkening of the sun on May 19, 1780, and the
meteoric shower on November 13, 1833, seem to mark the end of the period
of tribulation predicted.

Matthew 24:5, 11 introduces a prediction of a different order. Adventists
connect these verses with the spirit of falsehood depicted in Revelation 13:11-
17. Thus while a genuine revival springs from the preaching of the three angels' messages in Revelation 14, a counterfeit revival also develops, spurred on
by the beast and his helpers (Rev. 13). The signs and wonders engendered by
the false revival will be remarkable. We are therefore encouraged to pray so
that "when the wonderful miracle-working power shall be displayed, and the
enemy shall come as an angel of light, [we] may distinguish between the genuine work of God and the imitative work of the powers of darkness."[8] As we
await the Advent we must keep our eyes open and our minds alert. With so
many false views about the signs of the times circling within Christendom itself, we should know what the Word of God teaches about last-day events. At
the same time we should not strain to find a sign of the end in every headline.
We must strike the right balance, avoiding fanaticism on the one hand and
complacency on the other.

Death and Resurrection

We often speak of the second coming of Christ as the blessed hope, the
crowning narrative to earth's history that restores a sense of meaning to a
seemingly chaotic world. The Second Advent also promises the hope of resurrection to a new state of existence with the risen Lord (see Job 19:23-27;
1 Thess. 4:13-16; 1 Cor. 15:23-25). But what is the biblical concept of the

resurrection and what does it mean for our understanding of death as a human experience?

The Bible teaches that in the resurrection God restores the "body" to life (Rom. 8:11; Phil. 3:20, 21). In other words, biblical resurrection is a bodily resurrection. Remember that when Christ was resurrected, the tomb was empty. But biblical resurrection is not the result of an eternal immortal soul reuniting with a new, physical body. In the Bible the word translated "soul" does not depict a self-subsistent, immortal entity. Scripture teaches that only God has immortality (1 Tim. 6:16) and an immortal soul in humans would mean that they have innate immortality. Neither is bodily resurrection the same as physical resuscitation, in which a person returns to life for a little while longer but is subject once again to death. Resurrection is God's supernatural answer to the problem of death. By it the resurrected body, while sharing a connection with the old (the scars were present when Jesus was resurrected), undergoes a transformation that makes it incorruptible (1 Cor. 15:52-54).

Science has tried for years to identify and unlock the key to immortality. Procedures and experiments such as cryonics have demonstrated humanity's desperate desire to cheat death and live forever. But the Bible has already identified the key to eternal life. Christ's death and resurrection broke death's power and made the promise of human resurrection sure (Rom. 6:9). By Christ's victory over death, we too can be resurrected into a new life, but only if we remain in Him (2 Tim. 1:8-10; Rom. 6:23). For those who die in Christ before His return, resurrection will not be at death but when He comes the second time, at the "last trumpet" (1 Cor. 15:51-54). Jesus said, "I am the resurrection and the life. He who believes in Me will live even if he dies" (John 11:25, NASB). That is a promise to live by.

---

[1] *The SDA Bible Commentary*, vol. 4, p. 291.

[2] E. G. White, *The Desire of Ages*, p. 25.

[3] Actually, the book of Hebrews describes Jesus' intercessory work in the heavenly sanctuary in language reminiscent of the daily services of the earthly sanctuary (Heb. 7:26, 27).

[4] J. B. Polhill, *Acts*, The New American Commentary (Nashville: Broadman and Holman Pub., 2001), vol. 26, p. 135.

[5] *Ibid.*

[6] *The SDA Bible Commentary*, vol. 6, p. 160.

[7] Ellen G. White, *Last Day Events* (Boise, Idaho: Pacific Press Pub. Assn., 1992), p. 168.

[8] *Ibid.*, p. 169.

Chapter 13

When All Things Become New

Introduction

The Second Advent will inaugurate a 1,000-year period preceding the creation of a new earth. It and its attendant new world order is, with apologies to Sir Thomas Moore, the true expression of the concept of utopia.[1] The regaining of a perfect, ideal world is, in a sense, the goal toward which the Godhead has been working since humanity's Fall in the Garden of Eden. When Christ's work for human salvation concludes, He will return with never-before-seen glory, resurrect the dead and translate the living, and take them to reign with Him for the 1,000 years. The start of the millennium will therefore begin humanity's first-ever taste of perfection since its fall in Eden.

Events Inaugurating the Millennium

If the millennium marks the beginning of utopia for God's people, the natural impulse is to figure out when it will begin. The millennium, as a concept, appears in Revelation 20. The events that inaugurate the start of the millennium are those that accompany the Second Coming, and Revelation 20 notes three such events: the first resurrection (verse 5), the binding of Satan (verse 3), and the desolation of the earth (verse 3).

To place these events in Revelation 20 in context, sometime *before* Jesus' second advent, Revelation predicts the work of three powers—the dragon, the beast, and the false prophet—to assemble the nations to oppose the work of Christ and His people (Rev. 16:13). At the time of Christ's coming (Rev. 19:11 and following) the nations gather to make war against Christ, and in the process the beast and the false prophet will be destroyed (Rev. 19:19, 20). The three events of Revelation 20 are therefore concerned to some degree with the fate of the third power, the dragon. While the dead in Christ are resurrected (here called the first resurrection, verse 5), the brightness of His coming slays the wicked, and the dragon (Satan) is captured and cast into the bottomless pit for 1,000 years "so he might not deceive the nations any longer" (verses 1-3, ESV). Many see a symbolic link between the "banishment" of the scapegoat on the Day of Atonement (Lev. 16:22) and Satan's imprisonment on earth during the millennium.

In the Midst of the Millennium

The events marking the inauguration of the millennium occur on the earth. The millennium itself takes place in heaven with Jesus, and the redeemed are comforted by His constant presence. During the millennium thrones are set, books are opened, and "the souls of those who had been beheaded for their witness to Jesus and for the word of God, who had not worshiped the beast or his image, and had not received his mark on their foreheads or on their hands" (Rev. 20:4, NKJV) participate in the action. As Adventists, we understand that the Bible does not teach the existence of separate, immortal, conscious souls. This text, instead, describes those who experienced the persecution portrayed in Revelation 12:17-13:18. At the Second Advent Christ raises them to life and they ascend to heaven (compare with 1 Thess. 4:15-17) to reign with Him.

Revelation. 20:4 draws our attention to another millennium event, the judgment committed to the saints. The concept of final judgment in the Bible is rich and multifaceted and requires careful explanation. The final judgment has three phases. The first is associated with Christ's priestly ministry in the heavenly sanctuary. Adventists call it the investigative phase of the final judgment. The second is the millennial review phase of the judgment referred to in Revelation 20:4 and 1 Corinthians 6:2, 3. During it the redeemed have an opportunity to examine God's ways and judgments toward those who chose to rebel.[2] The third phase of the final judgment is the executive aspect that leads to decisions about the fate of every player in the great controversy. The second phase of judgment is that which God commits to those "beheaded for their testimony to Jesus and for the word of God" (Rev. 20:4, NKJV). They are the resurrected redeemed, seated on thrones and given authority to reign "with Christ a thousand years" (verse 4, NIV). In the end their judgment will confirm the justness and righteousness of God.

Events at the End of the Millennium

Revelation 20:5, 7-11, and chapter 21 describe a sequence of events that marks the end of the millennium. First there occurs a resurrection of the dead. But it is not the return to life of the just. Rather, it describes another group and their fate: "the rest of the dead did not come to life until the thousand years were completed" (Rev. 20:5, NASB). The second resurrection is that of the wicked to face judgment (John 5:29; Rev. 20:13).

Next is Satan's freeing from his prison, an event linked closely to the resurrection of the rest of the dead who "did not live again until the thousand years were finished" (Rev. 20:5, NKJV). Satan, on his release, attempts one last assault on the City of God. His army is the universal multitude of the wicked as numerous as "the sand of the seashore," and aptly described as "Gog and Magog," a multitude of the deceived from the beginning of the world to its end (verse 8; cf. Eze. 38:2). This multitude, led by its demonic leader, attacks the city, the New Jerusalem, called the "camp of the saints and the beloved city" (verse 9, NKJV). But the assault proves in vain and ends in eternal defeat by the last, final event.

Revelation 20:9, 10 summarizes the destruction of Satan and sinners. While they encircle the New Jerusalem, fire flashes down from God out of heaven to destroy them. The destruction (introduced in verse 9 and repeated in verses 14, 15) takes place in the context of the final judgment. It is a judgment of universal proportions, for all appear before the great white throne and are judged out of the books. Scripture describes the extinction of the wicked as the "second death" (verse 6), an absolute, complete, and total destruction (cf. Matt. 10:28).[3] The application of the word "eternal," or "everlasting," to historical entities (humans) or perishable objects does not mean "never-ending." Scripture states that Sodom and Gomorrah suffered the vengeance of eternal fire (Jude 7), yet those cities are not burning today. It defies reason to suggest that human beings who are innately mortal can somehow attain a kind of immortality burning forever in hell![4]

The New Earth

Revelation 20 ends with the elimination of Satan and his hosts, and Revelation 21 opens with a vision of a new heaven and a new earth. This new reality is unveiled because "the first heaven and the first earth passed away" (Rev. 21:1, NASB). The word translated "new" in Revelation 21:1 emphasizes something that, having once existed, has now attained a new form or quality, rather than something brought into existence for the first time. The new heaven and new earth follow the "first." They are not a completely unique, never-before-seen "something." Rather, we find an implied connection between what once was and what is now to be. The new world will also be a tangible place, inhabited by real, physical beings. But its substance and quality will be different. While it will have within it shadows of the past, it will have attained a brand-new form that we can now only imagine.

When sin entered the world, it thwarted God's purpose for creation, and creation itself felt that frustration, groaning and longing for liberty to become what God intended (Rom. 8:20-22). When God creates the world new, it will realize that purpose, freeing creation from its present state of incompleteness and bringing it into conformity with God's design. The new earth will be a renewed one, purified by fire (2 Peter 3:10-13). The New Jerusalem will be a physical dwelling place (Rev. 21:24-26) inherited by the saints (Rev. 21:7) and not, as some attempt to argue, a symbol for God's saints.[5] It will be the capital city of the new earth. God will be its light so that it will have no need for sun or moon. It will be constructed with the finest of building materials: golden streets, jasper walls, foundations of precious gems. The river of life will flow from the throne of God, and the tree of life will grow on either side of the river (Rev. 21:11-22:5). The eternal home of the redeemed, it is the fulfillment of biblical promises (Matt. 5:5; John 14:1-3).

Our world, with all its imperfections, is an aberration—a perversion of God's original creation. But Jesus came to restore it to the perfection that He intended it to have. The beauty and glory pictured in the Bible and promised to the faithful is no fable. As hard as it may be for us to grasp, with only the broken world around us as a guide, a real and glorious inheritance awaits us. The present dark world is not the end. Because of Jesus, we have hope of a mind-blowing new beginning.

Life in the New Earth

Revelation 21:3 gives us the earliest glimpse of life in the new earth and God's central role in the new order. "The tabernacle of God is among men," the heavenly voice declares, "and He will dwell among them, and they shall be His people, and God Himself will be among them" (NASB). Understand that the new home will not be just for us—the God of the universe will live with us. The holy, transcendent Creator will abide with His redeemed people. Of course, God will forever remain distinct from creatures, but in the new earth the separation between God and humanity brought about by sin will be removed. True and complete fellowship with God will be a daily experience. It will feed a spirit of peace, love, harmony, and righteousness in all our relationships (Isa. 65:25; Rev. 22:3).

When God restores the earth, He will eradicate everything that is harmful. Decay, disease, death, and suffering will be a thing of the past (Rom. 8:21; Rev. 21:4). No temple will exist there (Rev. 21:22), because God and the Lamb, the beings represented by the earthly sanctuary, will live among us. The gates will never close, because no enemy will launch an attack, and all people will have immediate, unhindered access to God's presence. Finally, there will be nothing there that defiles, because the Lord will have brought sin to a complete and final end. This truth, both a promise and a warning, marks the end of the great controversy between good and evil. "Sin and sinners are no more. The entire universe is clean. One pulse of harmony and gladness beats through the vast creation. From Him who created all, flow life and light and gladness, throughout the realms of [unlimited] space. From the minutest atom to the greatest world, all things, animate and inanimate, in their unshadowed beauty and perfect joy, will declare that God is love."[6]

[1] Sir Thomas More (1478-1535), an English lawyer, author, and statesman, coined the word "utopia" to depict an ideal, imaginary island nation with a seemingly perfect sociopolitical and legal system. Not only have people attempted to create such a society—their imaginations have sought to craft fictional utopias in literature. The word "utopia" sometimes gets used pejoratively to denote the impossibility of such a perfect society, yet by and large humanity clings to the positive use of the term and continues to dream and work for utopia.

[2] In the previous chapter we noted that Scripture connects judgment with Christ's ministry in the heavenly sanctuary before the Second Advent. That judgment is different from the one in Revelation 20:4, which is really a fulfillment of Christ's promise in Matthew 19:28 and which corresponds to Paul's statement that the saints will judge the world (1 Cor. 6:2).

[3] The agency of this absolute destruction is the lake of fire. Verse 9 declares the wicked to be consumed, or "eaten up" (Greek *katesthio*), pointing to total annihilation, but in verse 10 we see them in a lake of fire, also described as "eternal," or "unquenchable," thus suggesting at first glance eternal torment.

[4] For some recent rethinking among Evangelicals in support of annihilationism, see *Christianity Today,* Mar. 31, 2011.

[5] D. E. Aune, *Revelation 17-22,* Word Biblical Commentary (Dallas: Word, Incorporated, 2002), vol. 52C, p. 1122.

[6] Ellen G. White, *The Great Controversy,* p. 678.